THE KI.. GODS AND COMMONERS

by

Martin Horan

WALTON

WS

SERVICES
LTD

THE KING'S, GOD'S AND COMMONERS.

FIRST PUBLISHED BY WALTON SERVICES LTD.,
2001.

ISBN 1-903791-006

Other books by Martin Horan:

Fanny Who?   (Local Biography)
Scottish Executions, Assassinations and Murders
Scottish Dates   (An outline of Scottish history)
Scottish Castles
The Little Book of Jewish Wisdom
Hame Thochts Frae Hame (comic verse and cartoons)

Cover design by Eugeniusz Jarych

Acknowledgements

I AM HONOURED to have been asked to write this small book on the *King's Theatre* for the King's Theatre Trust publishers. The book's existence is really due to the efforts and industry of the Trust people themselves. They have worked not only to keep the memory of the theatre alive but, through their influence, have striven to keep the building itself in the best possible state of conservation.

And thanks should go to the management of *Deja Vu*, till recently *Brannigan's*, who have remained in agreement with the Trust's aims and aspirations and have given members of the trust and me permission to visit the premises for inspection and photograph taking. Shona Duncan, their Assistant Manager, personally guided me around parts of the building not open to public access and also informed me that I, or anyone else involved in this project, was welcome to return for any further study. Her offer encouraged me greatly and deserves thanks.

I would also like to thank Mr Adam Swan of the Dundee City Council Planning Department for the information with which he supplied me regarding the architecture of James and Frank Thomson; the Dundee City Archivist, Iain Flett, for his assistance and valuable lead; the two daughters of Frank Thomson, Trixie and Gertie, for their time, hospitality and personal reminiscences and for supplying me with essential data otherwise unattainable; Bill Dow, a former Dundee physics teacher, for sharing his academic and "inside" knowledge of those men, regarding both their work and their personal lives (none of which I found in my own researching except for, at best, allusions by other writers in the field); and Mrs Margaret Kidd for contacting me with information relating to her father, Bill Rogers, the King's first conductor; Alistair Eberst for assistance and advice with word-processing and computing and always being available when needed; and Ewan Stirling for his involvement in the computing side of the cover design.

Further thanks go to those who run the King's Theatre Trust: Henny King, the first Chairperson; Anya Lawrence, Secretary; David Hewick, for his expertise in building preservation; Paul Iles, for his knowledge in running and managing theatres; Jimmy Smith of Jimmy Smith's Print shop for help with the Trust's newsletter; George Gall, of Greenfinch Design consultants, Dundee, for his help with artwork; and to my old pal Andy Murray Scott for bringing the Trust and me together, resulting in my receiving the commission to write the book.

I also thank the unseen helpers who are too numerous to be named here for their interest and enthusiasm, The Friends of the King's Theatre.

I would especially like to thank Iain and Stephen Fraser of the Trust for their patience and encouragement and whose encyclopaedic knowledge of the theatre I could turn to when needed. Their faith in my journalistic skills earned me the job. I hope the pages of this book live up to it.

Martin Horan

FOREWORD

I WELCOME THIS brief history of the King's Theatre, Dundee, sponsored by the King's Theatre Trust. Growing up in Dundee, I remember the shows there in the fifties and sixties, the last years it was in use as a theatre. I was pleased to become President of the King's Theatre Trust During the campaign to bring about its restoration. Although the campaign did not have enough time to attract the support needed for this, it did succeed in preventing Frank Thomson's lovely building being gutted and turned into shops. The building is now used as a nightclub by Brannigan's -- yet another form of entertainment. Perhaps a future generation will be able to make it a theatre again.

Over the last century, the King's Theatre has been used for everything ranging from music hall to opera, bands to bingo, cinema to nightclub. Martin Horan has managed to capture this, and pays tribute to the memory of the architect Frank Thomson. The building has a special place in the memories of Dundonians, and this valuable book will keep them alive.

Brian Cox

PREFACE

DUNDONIANS AND OTHER Taysiders of my generation -- those born between 1945 and 1955 -- can remember with fondness the *Gaumont* cinema.

The building still stands in the city's Cowgate, East of Panmure Street. In there we saw films which made lasting impressions on our minds. They go right across the board: from Ealing comedies to Hammer horrors, from Bible epic to James Bond thrillers. Three of Hollywood's greatest musicals, *The Sound of Music, Mary Poppins* and *Fiddler on the Roof,* made their Dundee débuts there. It was also the cinema where countless thousands of children from Dundee and environs spent their Saturday mornings enjoying the matinées. After the Second World War the children sang the club songs in tune with the organ playing of "Aunty Cathie."

Of course, similar claims can be made for other Dundee cinemas that showed the same kind of films. They also had matinées where the above generations of children saw the same kinds of Saturday serials, comedies and cartoons. So why should the memory of the *Gaumont* -- better known to our parents and grandparents as the *Kings* -- be upheld before any other Dundee cinema? And why should Dundonians be minded to care about preserving the interior of a building that no longer serves the use for which it was built?

These are fair enough questions. They deserve to be answered.

Regarding Dundee cinemas, the *Gaumont* had a unique history. It was last to do children's Saturday matinées. And it was the last to double as a live theatre and a cinema. The fact that it wasn't just a cinema but was by far the best theatre in the city is an even better reason.

Its conception and construction was connected with an important family of Dundee architects, the Thomsons, also largely forgotten for their contribution. Two prominent members of that family were sadly and unfairly maligned.

Though, of course, when they were involved with the building, it was to be known by its original name of the *Kings and Hippodrome.* Dundonians simply called it the *King's.* That was the actual name on the building from the outset. It was a name that also stuck. When it was renamed *Gaumont* older Dundonians continued to call it the *King's.* A similar thing happened with people of my generation. They still refer to it as the *Gaumont* though it was called the *Odeon* for the last years of its existence as a cinema.

7

But it is as the *King's* it deserves to be remembered. Those were truly its glory years

It also served an important contribution to the planning of the city centre and to Dundee itself as an important metropolis. No other Dundee theatre or cinema has done so in that manner. And, besides, it greatly served the social needs of that time in the way not applicable to any other cinema and/or theatre.

Some of the original interior is still intact and *Deja Vu* are pleased with it being maintained. (The name was recently changed from *Brannigan's* to *Deja Vu*. [See acknowledgements.] I have been informed that new alterations are being made. The company is under the same management, *First Leisure*.) Sadly, due to the wanton vandalism in 1961 that passed off for modernisation, the auditorium was virtually destroyed. Though the "oval" ceiling is preserved above a false ceiling.

There are extant records showing that Dundee had theatres and cinemas with sumptuous interiors worthy of any European capital. Indeed, a couple of those interiors are well within living memory. The latter, though, is only in the cases of cinemas such as the *Green's Playhouse* and, that Art Deco wonder, the long since demolished *Odeon*. It stood in Strathmartine Road, adjacent to Coldside Library -- incidently another building connected to the same Thomsons. (There were other Art Deco cinemas, such as the *Empire* in Rosebank Street and the *Rex* in Alexander Street. But -- and here I am relying on memory -- in my opinion these were nowhere in the class of the *Odeon*.)

In the last chapter of his book *Records of the Dundee Stage* (published by W & D.C. Thomson in 1886), Frank Boyd gives a detailed description of the "new" *Her Majesty's Theatre and Opera House*:

"...Round the centre doorway runs a very richly carved architrave, in the centre of which is a cartouche with the pot and lilies of the town. On each side of the doorway is a double-fluted pilaster, with moulded bands, from which spring boldly-treated trusses, supporting a projecting balcony, with balustrade and carved vases at the corners. The truss towards the High Street bears a medallion portrait of Shakespeare, and the companion truss to the eastward has a similar likeness of Mozart..."

Boyd continues to describe almost every nook and cranny of the elaborate Victorian theatre. But his description testifies to the fact that Dundee had such sumptuous theatres. Though the feature that truly impressed Boyd was its "central illuminant" of which he says "burn no less than one hundred and seventy-one jets". *Her Majesty's*, which was estimated at a cost of £12,000 to build -- an enormous sum then -- was gutted by a fire, eventually making way for the *Capitol* to be erected on the grounds. That meant there were no theatres of international standard

8

left in Dundee, except for the *King's*.

The only other playhouse that came remotely near to that standard was the *Green's Playhouse*. However, that only served as a cinema. And those which had been converted from theatres to cinemas were not to the standard of interior decoration as the *King's*. The actors, singers, and dancers who appeared and continued to appear on stage there, until it became a full-time cinema, were of international reputation. Again, this put the *King's* beyond the par of any other Dundee theatre.

The Caird Hall (another Thomson creation) equals it in the way of the famous conductors, musicians, etc., who appeared there. But, despite the fact that it is an incredible building in itself, it was never intended to be a theatre. Besides, the Caird Hall is still serving the uses for which it was built -- concerts and public meetings.

So, the only building we had in the city, built to be and still usable as a theatre of international standing and interior excellence, was the (then named) *Gaumont* -- till its "modernisation" in 1961. These are excellent reasons for preserving and restoring.

Due to the above wanton vandalism fobbed off as an excuse for modernisation, and the further destruction that took place when the place was turned into a bingo hall, the proscenium arch, the pit, adjacent opera box walls and the panel walls of the auditorium are beyond repair. The Baroque style balcony fronts of the middle and upper circles were also destroyed in 1961. King's Theatre enthusiasts can only hope against hope that one day these things can be restored. Fortunately, there is no reason why the "oval" ceiling (which is actually round) cannot be conserved.

There is little left of old Dundee. The Overgate was bulldozed in the sixties to make way for the Angus Hotel and shopping precinct. But did it in any way *really* improve the centre? The fact that the Angus Hotel has itself been demolished and most of the precinct has been chopped and changed beyond recognition answers that question.

The erection of Kirk Style and the "New" Overgate meant demolishing buildings of local historical note -- viz., Camperdown Land (built to commemorate Admiral Duncan's famous victory), Monk's Land along with the other adjoining buildings forming the "island" between Thorter Row, The High Street and Overgate. This followed a pattern of Dundee demolition. First in 1777 when the city fathers consented to the razing of James Mylne's Mercat Cross (to the eternal destruction of the unicorn -- the present one is a replica -- and the crenellated town crier's platform) and, in 1872 the Reform Hall. At least when the Trades Hall, at the opposite end of the High Street was demolished in 1878 they opened the vista to a building of practical and architectural significance.

Same goes for the old Town House, known locally as "the Pillars", and the Vault, the area behind it, over which the present City Square was built. The Baroque Town House was designed by the renowned William Adam. Still, it was replaced by something arguably both more aesthetic and functional. Even so, there was an outcry at the time. But to no avail though many Dundonians were to lament the demolition for decades. The name of the Pillars bar on Crichton Street, and the replica Town House above its doorway, attest to that nostalgia, as does the replica on the clock in the High Street.

Granted, it was not feasible that the Town House and the other buildings in the Vault area could have been conserved, as explained later in the book. But, lamentably, it was an old part of the town we lost. And we've since lost other old parts we needn't have. The great cities of Europe have their "old towns" -- the quarters dating from medieval and Renaissance times. No Continental town planners would dare to suggest the demolition of those areas. The very idea is laughable. Europeans put us to shame when it comes to preserving their buildings and keeping alive the memory of their architects.

The points I'm making are, we have lost much already in Dundee -- albeit that much of the demolition was necessary -- and, if we have a will to, we can not only hold on to our heritage but we can restore what's been lost. We have all but lost the *King's Theatre*, other than its outer casing, and a few other excellent parts of the interior. If the powers that be in Dundee had the wit to see it, they would be ashamed of the situation. They ought to have set an example.

We have much to be grateful to the King's Theatre Trust for. Their campaign was one of the most effective and disciplined campaigns Dundee had seen. It started in 1994 soon after County Bingo's announcement that the building was to be sold. A small group of public-spirited individuals decided it should be restored to expand the range of live entertainment in the city.

They were quick to achieve much. The King's Theatre Trust was formed. Brian Cox undertook to be President and Richard Demarco, James Donald (formerly manager of His Majesty's Theatre in Aberdeen), Sir James Dunbar-Nasmyth (the architectural historian), Stephen Fry (then Rector of Dundee University) and the writer Billy Kay agreed to become patrons. Local businessman George Gall provided them with a professionally produced logo and letterhead.

Fund-rasing followed and market research was commissioned -- showing there were indeed gaps in the market. And the results were used as part of a submission for the local economic development plan, Scottish Enterprise Tayside, and subsequently as part of the Dundee Performing Arts Study.

A public meeting was held in the Marryat Hall in December 1995, attracting

150 people. It resulted in gaining the support of the Theatres Trust. From there they went on to organizing fund-raising events. They included a cabaret evening with Lesley Mackie and George Donald and an evening with Billy Kay, based on his book *Knee Deep in Claret.*

After the Trust gave a presentation, KMPG provided generous help with the business plan. Paul Isles, the then manager of Edinburgh's Festival Theatre contributed expertise from the sharp end of business. My informant also tells me that "Paul Iles was a tower of strength throughout the campaign."

Newsletters and summary copies of the business plan were sent to every councillor. A particular achievement (among the many) worth noting was that the developer who had acquired the building withdrew his plans to gut the theatre and turn it into shops.

The campaign gathered momentum. This was despite lack of encouragement from the city council. They had already committed funds to the building of the Contemporary Arts Centre.

Awaiting news of their lottery bid, the Trust were informed that the building was to be bought for use as a theme pub/night club. Their advisers explained that it would be a far more difficult option to oppose on planning grounds. In August 1997, First Leisure, then owner of the *Brannigan's* brand of theme pubs, was granted planning permission and took over the building.

But the Trust had received commitments from the Scottish Arts Council, and other bodies, towards further studies of Dundee's needs. Consequently, the Dundee Performing Arts Study was carried out. It involved members of their -- the Trust's -- steering committee and Dundee council officials. And the results helped prepare the way for improvements to the local performing arts programme.

Their campaign ended soon afterwards. But not without success. They achieved something unexpected and worthy of praise from all Dundonians. It was discovered that First Leisure had actually restored a large part of the original premises. That means conversion of the building back to its original purpose is still a future possibility. Perhaps then, some day, Frank Thomson will cease to remain an underestimated architect whose work has so far been neglected.

Such funds that were left were split between two good causes -- to sponsor this book (!) and to contribute to the Whitehall Theatre Trust. The Trust themselves want me to pass on their gratitude to those who have helped them -- though it is impossible here for me to name them all. Two thousand people are on the mailing list, so it speaks for itself.

Picture A

KINGS THEATRE, DOVER

INTRODUCTION TO THE HISTORY OF DUNDEE THEATRE

A CURSORY READING of Dundee's history would give the impression that we have a long-standing tradition of dramatic appreciation.

Understandable, when there is reasonable assumption -- though no concrete proof to back it -- that Shakespeare and his company of players visited the town. Not only did the immortal Edmund Kean act in our first theatre but his Shylock, reputed to be the greatest, was based on that of Dundee's most famous actor of the day. And arguably two of the greatest playwrights in the English language visited Dundee -- Oscar Wilde and William Butler Yeats. Wilde lectured at the Theatre Royal on Friday, 20th October 1883 and Yeats lectured on Thursday, 12th January 1906, at University College.

And Tyrone Power was a Dundonian!

The first attempts at theatre in Dundee occurred during the Middle Ages. These were the performances of the miracle and morality plays. They took place in the open countryside on the edge of the towns, in allocated areas called playfields

Dundee's playfield was called Westfield, otherwise Mains of Dudhope. It was just outside the town wall at the Argyle (now West) Port. There was a spot nearby called Witches' Knowe. From its grassy slopes the audiences watched the miracle and morality plays.

(Witches' Knowe was where the road now runs from the roundabout at the Blackness Road/Horsewater Wynd intersection to the West Port. As a sixteenth century map of Dundee shows, Westfield must have sloped from that part down towards what is now the Guthrie Street-Lochee Road area. Somewhere in that vicinity, possibly covered by a former jute mill, the plays were performed.)

Miracle and morality plays were not the same thing. Miracle plays dealt with events from the Bible, with themes ranging from the Creation account to the Last Judgement. The later ones, based on lives of the saints and the Virgin Mary, are more correctly called mystery plays because of the miraculous content.

Morality plays were not so overtly religious. The themes of those were more of human virtue and vice and usually personified in allegorical characters. To an extent they were developments of the miracle plays. The miracle plays were the earliest but both were performed over the same periods during the late Middle Ages.

Still, the morality plays were obviously palatable enough for the clergy in Dundee as elsewhere. Drama in the conventional sense was frowned upon by them. The staging of the miracle and morality plays, on the other hand, was a way of educating an illiterate populace in things pertaining to Scripture and doctrine. Clergymen would normally have written the plays as very few others were literate.

The mystery plays relating to the Virgin Mary would have been popular with the townsfolk. She was Dundee's patron saint, thus the name of its main church and the opening words of the *Magnificat* being the university's motto. Dundee had enough influential religious powers to commend and encourage the local Mariolatry.

The Dundee Guild system, Scotland's earliest, flourished from the twelfth century and its craftsmen and tradesmen supplied some of the players. The guild members who performed in Westfield, sometimes on open wagons, would have done so out of religious conviction and civic and family pride.

The honour would have been similar to that of having a family member as a church altar assistant or chorister. Church processions were as common in Dundee as elsewhere in Scotland till the early seventeenth century. And just as it was a matter of family pride to have relatives walking in those processions, it would have been so for those who had them performing in the miracle and morality plays. Processions through the streets on saints days not only venerated the saints but included carrying the banners of the crafts and guilds. That meant the craftsmen and tradesmen could march and show off their importance in medieval society.

Pigs had the run of the Dundee streets until 1591 and their swill troughs were everywhere. Bodily effluences were dumped onto open middens already full of rotten vegetable peelings, discarded fish parts, poultry guts and various entrails. These were often piled against the townsfolk's dwellings. So, a church procession, or a miracle play performed in a field, would have been a colourful and dramatic event. Each Holy Day for the average person was an escape from the daily grind of work. Jesters, acrobats, conjurers, minstrels, drummers and pipers added to the entertainment. P.D. Torrie in his *Medieval Dundee* gives a surviving list of the materials, hardware and costumes used for a *Corpus Christi* celebration:

> ...sixte of crownis, six pair of angel reynis [wings], thre myteris, cristis cott
> [coat] of lethyr with the hoses and glufis, cristis hed, thirtie one suerdis, thre
> lang corsis of tre [wood], sanc thomas sper, a cors til sanc blasis, sanc johnis
> coit, a credil and thre barnis maid of clath, twentie hedis of hayr, the four

evangellistis, sanc katernis wheil...

It shows the guilds were willing to spend a great deal on these celebrations.

The May Revels were popular. These were presided over by the Abbot of Unreason, a kind of king of fools. Everyone acted a part where society was virtually turned on its head. In some places in Scotland Robin Hood was lord of the games. He caught on in Dundee, the furthest North he went in the country. Legend has him as the Earl of Huntingdon -- the title of the founder of Dundee. Whether this was the reason he was chosen can only be a guess. But by the time those events were being chronicled, the Dundee burgesses were appointing Robin Hood to lead the revels -- for which he was given a free burgess-ship!

Anyway, the Reformation put an end to these annual revels here as elsewhere.

The nearest other thing the populace had to open-air theatre was the burning of witches and the hanging, flogging and branding of convicted criminals. And the punishment for less serious crimes provided some lighter entertainment. Crowds laughed and jeered at those with their ears nailed to the tron, who were locked in the stocks, or who crawled on their knees through town, their ankles tied with a rosary.

Yet, we should not overlook the influence of the miracle and morality plays on our first writers of drama though those "plays" were simply written and with no real structure. They gave our first dramatists a concept of how to relate to their audiences. The art of acting developed from those same beginnings.

Dundee's first play, in the sense of a conventional drama, was written by James Wedderburn. *The Tradgedie of St John the Baptist*, as it was called, was first performed in 1540 in Westfield. The scant documentation we have of his other plays insinuate they were far from religious in tone. One, *The Comedie of Dionysius the Tyrant*, was performed "on the open space to the north of the Witches Know."

The first reference to any theatrical performance in Dundee's history (quoted from the manuscript volume of the earliest burgh records) states:

13th September, 1553. The quhilk day Elspeth Kymonthe is adjugit
to delyver to Jhone Fothringhame his trumpat quhilk ye said Jhone Fothringhame lent to ye said Elspeth Kinmonthe in ye time of ye play at ye Westfield.

The Westfield play was likely one of Wedderburn's.

Some assume Shakespeare visited Dundee about half a century later. This is due to Elizabeth I sending the Lawrence Fletcher Company of London actors to James VI's court in Edinburgh. Shakespeare was known to be associated with them. There was a chance he was with them as there was equally a chance that he was not. As the troupe are reported as having played in Edinburgh and Aberdeen, it's then assumed that they stopped at Dundee for a rest and further assumed that they would have acted there. It proves nothing either way. But it *is* an interesting theory!

Despite Royal approval, the clergy openly voiced their hostile opinions against performances and performers -- as an ecclesiastical pamphlet of the times testifies:

> It is agreed upon by sober pagans themselves that play-actors are the most profligate wretches and vilest vermin that Hell ever vomited out, that are the filth and garbage of the earth, the scum and stain of human nature, the pests and plague of society, the debauchers of men's minds and morals, unclean beasts, idolatrous papists or atheists and the most horrid and abandoned villains that ever the sun shone upon!

Perhaps the Clergy recalled how playwrights ridiculed the Catholic Clergy and consequently usurped *their* authority. But they need not have worried. The general public had a superstitious reverence for the Protestant ministry as it had in earlier times for the Catholic priesthood. This most likely accounted for almost universal hostility towards actors. An incident in the area during that period illustrates the point: Some fisherfolk of Broughty Ferry pleaded with the Town Council to expel a troupe. They believed their presence was the reason for God's wrath on the community -- as divinely expressed via depleted shoals in the Tay estuary.

Nothing else occurs drama-wise in Dundee until 1734. But attitudes eventually mellowed to some extent over those years. A company visited the burgh through the encouragement of the poet Allan Ramsay. The players received a grand reception. A holiday was declared and the Freemasons, led by the Grand Master and accompanied by the town officials, "marched in procession to the playhouse dressed in all their proper vestments and with hautboys and other instruments." The procession itself would have been a theatrical event, reminiscent of the church ones prior to the Reformation.

There is nothing on record as to where the "playhouse" was situated nor any hint of what kind of building it was. But all chronicled information on the play suggest that it was performed inside a building. And what *is* on record, though, is that one of the plays presented was *The Devil to Pay* or *The Wives Metamorphosed* So we can state with certainty that one of the first known staged plays in Dundee was a comedy by Charles Coffey, a successful Irish playwright who died in 1745.

About another twelve years passed before anything else theatrical occurred in Dundee. An extant playbill tells us that two plays were performed (*gratis*) at the Dundee Town House on Monday evening of May 26th, 1755. The first play was Charles Farquhar's *The Recruiting Officer* and the other a Henry Fielding adaption of Molière. The same company played a week earlier in a play called *George Barnwell*, written by George Lillo. Posterity has not been so kind to the other play.

The fact that it took so long for a company to come to Dundee shows that the Clergy's influence was persuasive. An Act was passed in 1737 licensing the stage.

The measure was retrogressive for the theatre, as shown in the playbill mentioned above. It advertises a concert with two plays thrown in for free. The subterfuge was to avoid paying licence fees. And perhaps to appease the Clergy and their followers -- who did not consider concerts as much of a vice as playgoing. The company did manage to fool the Clergy and the law enforcers for nearly two months, staging other plays in their run. The most notable was Gay's *Beggar's Opera*.

In 1767 comedians from Edinburgh's Theatre Royal were given a licence to play in the Dundee "Town Hall." They played in a tragedy, curiously enough, called Jane Shore, by Nicholas Rowe. It was followed by a farce called *Lethe*. In 1778 several plays were performed in the main chamber of the Trades Hall.

There is an interesting point about the Trades Hall building. After its demolition, a painting that hung inside it was saved. Painted by Alexander Methven, a local housepainter and amateur artist, it tells of a part of Dundee's theatrical history of which much has been lost:

The shoemakers were one of the nine incorporated trades represented in the Trades Hall. They had processions in Dundee, as in other towns, which finished with street theatre. Methven has given us some idea of what these processions and plays were like. His painting, a long frieze, depicts various members of the guilds marching, some carrying banners and flags. The Deacons and Past Deacons of Trade are dressed in white suits. There are also equestrian characters. One is a turbaned Moor in dark make-up, the other a knight in armour. The main character, enthroned, is King Crispin. They culminated in some kind of mock battle-cum-play.

These processions and plays took place on St Crispin's day, till the Reformation stopped them. They were very rarely revived. Though the saint became king he was still highly suspect. In October of 1882 (presumably 25th) one King Crispin's day was revived. It was the last.

Anyway, 1778 was an exceptional year for Dundee theatre. After that the records are silent till 1784 when a Mr Jackson of the Edinburgh Theatre Company arranged to play for a season in Dundee. The Town Council, taking a grim view of the matter convened on August 9th to " unanimously resolve by every legal means to oppose Mr Jackson and his company in exhibiting plays here".

As performances started to take place quite openly in Dundee in the latter part of the eighteenth century, there was obviously a growth in public demand for more theatre. As the nineteenth century approached the Clergy got less of their own way and eventually a permanent theatre for the town was a reality.

Dundee's first theatre was opened on 23rd July 1800. It stood in Yeaman Shore where it projected onto Craig Pier. The pier was in the vicinity of the present railway station. A promontory jutted into the Tay. It housed a timber yard and a granary. The granary became the theatre and local wits claimed that the lingering smell of fermenting grain was its main attraction.

The situation of the Theatre Royal, as it was named, was far from salubrious. Robertson was blunt: "The surrounding area was the home of the riff-raff who infested the water front and the only direct access from the High Street was by two narrow lanes...narrow evil ways...Thieves and pick-pockets were doubtless in attendance"

Nevertheless, reports from the time say the theatre was "fitted up in a very elegant and superior style." But for those sophisticates who loved theatre or wanted to experience playgoing, there was no option but to brave the environment.

The two men who founded the theatre, Messrs Moss and Bell were certainly enterprising. And their willingness to take the incredible risk paid off. Initially.

The play on the opening night was *The Merchant of Venice.* Shylock was played by Moss himself, whose performances of the role inspired the young Edmund Kean. Kean, the most renowned Shylock, saw Moss playing it in 1805 in Dumfries and was enthralled. He also acted at the Theatre Royal where they must have met. Moss in his younger days seemed headed for greater things. He had been the toast of Edinburgh, Dublin and London. *There* he played at the Haymarket Theatre. But things were rarely easy for him. Prior to visiting Dundee he opened a theatre in Whitehaven. About a week later, on a Saturday, the troupe were arrested and imprisoned. The following Monday they were denounced in the court as "a curse to society in general, but to Whitehaven in particular". Then another accusation was made: "Before the theatre opened, there was an immense intake of herrings. But since the players entered the town they have all fled and the fishermen are now suffering."

The accuser also claimed that actors bring curses wherever they go. The court agreed, shut down the theatre and expelled the "sons of the Wicked One." Perhaps they'd heard the story of actors depleting the fish stocks in the Tay estuary!

Moss and Bell produced a comedy by a local author in 1802. Though there is no documentation of his name there is of the play. It was called *The Pretty Girl of Dundee,* But the characters weren't too parochial. One was a farmer from faroff Longforgan! Called Grump to boot.

The audiences by then were no longer the discerning educated classes. For the first couple of years of the theatre's existence they had seen several acting greats, including John Kemble and Henry Johnston. But within four years a new clientele was watching tightrope acts and prizefighting. Daniel Mendoza, the most famous of those barefist boxers appeared there.

The new clientele came in larger numbers. Bell was more happy with the arrangement than Moss. *He* left for Dumfries after being only three years in Dundee. Perhaps this was more to do with Moss taking his acting more seriously than Bell. Bell is on record only as making a few narrations on stage.

Though there are no exact recorded dates of when the theatre closed, it was likely before the new one opened. Probably before 1808 when "Mr Samuel Bell [an architect] was instructed to prepare plans for a theatre in Castle Street." (He was no relation to the other Bell.) We also know that after the theatre closed there was

...a building near the top of New Inn Entry on the West side, where plays were sometimes presented. Little is known about this place except that it had previously been a place of worship...

New Inn Entry, now called Chapel Street, runs from the (Arctic Bar) pend opposite the City Square to Meadowside. The building to the West of the North end, facing the Albert Institute, is mentioned as a Gaelic chapel on a 1910 map.

The new Theatre Royal opened on June 27th (1810). The original edifice still stands on the east side of Castle Street. The bust of Shakespeare in the pediment reminds us of its original function. But the ground floor, now home to the Tourist Board, housed shops from the outset. Thomas Hood refers to it in a derisory poem he wrote of Dundee in 1815: For beneath a Theatre or Chapel they'll pop/ A saleroom, a warehouse, a mean little shop. The shops, though, were quite classy. Their windows were Roman arched, some with keystones, and separated with Roman Doric pilasters. Ornate lantern lamps hung from above them.

The first manager of the Castle Street theatre was Henry Siddons. He was the son of Sarah Kemble, a well-known actress who had eight siblings all of whom were equally well-known actors/actresses.

Siddons brought an Edinburgh company to the Theatre Royal. His wife was one of the members. She was given a role in a comedy called *The West Indian* and another in a following farce called *Fortune's Frolic*. She was a talented actress and her leading man was Daniel Terry. He was equally talented and became famous throughout Scotland. Sir Walter Scott was his close friend.

The above were the first plays acted in a permanent theatre in Dundee. But they were not staged till weeks after the opening. As Robertson comments: "It is rather typical of Dundee's abortive enthusiasm that the new theatre was not even opened with an impressive dramatic production, but with a benefit concert by the band of the Forfarshire Local Militia, and it was not until two months after the opening date that the first run of a play was presented."

The audiences certainly paid for their privileges: Box seats two shillings, the pit one shilling, the gallery sixpence. This was a considerable sum for the time -- especially as the majority who were in the pit had to stand. Often they were crammed together. But people were more easily pleased then. They may have stood in the gallery also. But there could have been benches there. The gallery held 500 and the pit 420. Though one estimate suggested that, at a push, the theatre could hold a maximum of twelve hundred.

After the comedy run, Siddons' uncle -- Stephen Kemble -- introduced a Shakespearian season. It started on September 3rd. He played Falstaff and was fat enough not to need padding for the part. But his success at the part was due more to his excellent acting than his obesity.

The Shakespeare experiment soon ran its course and within a year the theatre was staging more popular entertainment. In spite of that, it still struggled. To make matters worse, Siddon died. He left his family in penury and W.H. Murray took command of his affairs. He was a younger member of the company. But he could only open the theatre for brief seasons. The Edinburgh Company was to appear there on Friday October 4th, 1816. This was billed as being for the last time under Murray's management.

The show included a comedy and a farce plus "Singing, dancing, &c., and a grand naval and national selection of ballads, called 'British Tars or Saturday Night at Sea,' the last scene of which represents a great panoramic view of the city of Algiers, with the destruction of the fleet and batteries of the Allied Squadron." But though it was a kind of entertainment for the masses for that period, it didn't really draw them. The public demand for a permanent theatre had waned rapidly.

But Murray wasn't a quitter. He tried again, getting the company to perform a "Positively last night" under his management. This was on the 25th October and it was a flop. And it brought the miserable season to its end.

The following August a quarter of the building was offered for sale. It had been vacant for a year. At some point part of it was used as a waxworks museum. Occasionally one-off concerts and variety entertainment events were produced there. It was also used for "the examination of the deaf and dumb scholars of the town..."

The theatre was to receive a stroke of luck in 1818 with the staging of a new play. It was called *Rob Roy MacGregor* or *Auld Langsyne,* and was a "hit" for its time. It was produced by the company of the leading actor, Corbet Ryder, making him a celebrity throughout Scotland. It also netted £3,000 for Murray.

In 1819 a typhoid epidemic struck Dundee. The Theatre Royal hosted a benefit concert for the victims and raised 75 guineas. A fortune then for a one-off performance. But, by that time, Ryder and his players were struggling because the audiences were dwindling. Eventually Ryder left for Edinburgh to work at the Caledonia Theatre. He returned in 1820 to perform briefly in July.

On the 17th "the greatest phenomenon of the age" Clara Fisher appeared for the first time in Dundee. She was only nine. As a six-year old infant she performed Richard III at Drury lane! During her Theatre Royal run, she played Richard III, Falstaff and Dr Pangloss. Local critics went into ecstasies over her performances.

She was succeeded by Charles Mayne Young who played for five nights, the first as Hamlet. He was another eminent actor, well-known for his appearances at Covent Garden. But for all the great acting on offer there were few takers. In August 1820, the *Dundee Advertiser* commented that "the people of Dundee are so destitute of dramatic taste that one wonders if it would not be advisable for all parties that the theatre should never open again."

I mentioned earlier that Tyrone Power was a Dundonian. At least the *original* one was. (Or he acted here. His nativity remains uncertain.) He was one of Ryder's troupe. Admittedly, he was *then* billed as Thomas Power. But he was to become a stage Irishman and command the absolute fortune of £150 per week -- the highest salary ever paid till then to a comedian. He played at London's Haymarket and visited America twice. According to the late David Phillips (a Dundee writer who wrote on local subjects) *that* Tyrone Power was the great-great grandfather of his namesake the American film star.

Robertson appears to mix him up with the great Dundee actor Tom Powrie. Phillips, in his book *Lichty Nichts Omnibus*, includes a chapter to Powrie -- who made his début as a schoolboy in the mid 1830s acting in stables next to his mother's house at 120 Nethergate. His début on real stage was in the Yeaman Shore building. He played the main role of Richard III there a year before it had been bought over by the railway company. He also played in the Theatre Royal, the Thistle and Cooke's Circus.

He became one of Scotland's most popular actors, dying in Edinburgh in 1869. His body was brought to Dundee where a large crowd followed the cortège to the Western Cemetery. His remains lie there in an unmarked grave.

By the early 1820s things had been going badly for Dundee drama. For most of the time the Theatre Royal was empty. Few companies would chance it. And, to make matters worse, the Caledonian Hall opened nearby -- in Castle Street itself. Though only concerts were held there, it became a serious rival for potential musical productions.

But the Theatre Royal management did occasionally procure popular entertainers. In July 1824 Alexandre the ventriloquist performed there several times. According to Boyd, he was one of the most successful solo entertainers who ever lived. Walter Scott mentions him in a poem. He was a bit of a practical joker but proved less troublesome than the celebrated Sinclair.

Sinclair was a vocalist who Ryder managed to entice to appear the following September. He was famed throughout Europe as an operatic singer but was a bit of a *prima donna*. While singing an aria in the Theatre Royal, he abruptly stopped. Subsequently, the curtain fell. This infuriated Sinclair who accused the orchestra of incompetency. The incident added to the theatre's troubles.

In November of 1831 Paganini came to Dundee. He was booked to play there. But an open dispute occurred between the manager and the owners. The manager had fallen behind with arrears in rent so the concert was cancelled. As Paganini was about to depart Dundee, he was pleaded with to give a concert elsewhere. He gave two -- apparently in the Caledonian Hall.

In July the following year officers of the 71st regiment performed in Colman's *Ways and Means* to raise money for the poor. Two and a half years later some players tried to get a regular pantomime off the ground. To no avail. It looked as if the Theatre Royal was finished. Dundonians had lost all interest in theatre. On the 17th, 18, and 19 of February 1835, the management tried to entice the public with two popular performers. The scheme didn't work. The theatre closed.

The locals were preferring the alternative entertainment offered in a hall in the Meadows -- the present Meadowside area. Two records mention Cooke's Circus and Ord's Circus being in that area. But not in detail. Though the already mentioned Gaelic chapel looked into the Meadows, the circus wasn't the same building.

In January of 1838 some kind of performance took place in the Theatre Royal. The most eventful thing about it was that a member of the audience fell asleep and was locked in. He awoke at 4 a.m. His hammering and shouting wasn't heard till about four hours later. The following month some kind of equestrian events were held there. The place wasn't suitable for horses so it was another flop.

Despite the dire circumstances of the Theatre Royal another had opened in Yeaman Shore. It was called the Royal Shakespeare Pantheon and was a nearby neighbour to Messrs Moss and Bell's building. It had only been open for about a year when tragedy struck. But it was far more dramatic than anything ever produced there.

On the evening of June 28th of the same year, a crowd of Dundee youths got carried away with the celebrations for Queen Victoria's coronation. As evening approached, palings marking off street boundaries were heaped to make bonfires in the High and adjacent streets. The police tried to intervene but the crowds were uncontrollable.

A crowd of young men went to the King William dock and seized a boat placed on the quay. They poured tar into it and set it alight. Somehow, the mob managed to drag the blazing thing past St Mary's churches and down Union Street to Yeaman Shore. They then suggested setting Cooke's Circus on fire. But the ringleader, named David Lyon, realized the mob -- now numbering around five thousand -- would be unlikely to follow a burning boat up to the Meadows. So he burst open the doors of the Pantheon and threw some burning palings inside. Another report claims the fire started through sparks catching some wax effigies on the edifice of the wooden structure. Being highly inflammable they soon had the Pantheon more ablaze than the boat.

All reports say the mobs enjoyed the spectacle. Whatever the truth of it being started deliberately, there was general assent that public morality would benefit from the destruction of the place. It *was* a theatre after all. And David Lyon was gaoled for a year. His fellow ringleaders were also gaoled for eight and four months respectively. So their judge and jury reckoned them deliberate arsonists.

The irony was that the Pantheon was a popular place with Dundee's young people. They favoured its "strong and often equally broad drama." Yet the youth were to be its undoing, making it the shortest-lived theatre ever in Dundee. Another was built by Jamie Scott, the proprietor, and survived as a permanent circus. (Circus was often the name for a theatre that was simply circular or nearly circular -- as in Cooke's and/or Ord's. Sometimes it could be a theatre with both a stage and a ring, in which the seating could be arranged depending on the entertainment. But the ring sometimes included some kind of animal act. And they could host trapeze artists, acrobats and jugglers.)

The Dundee public had again been clamouring for another theatre about that time. That's what makes the reaction to the fire seem contradictory. It was the public demand for more theatre in the first place that encouraged enthusiasts like Scott to open one. Obviously there were two sizeable opposing factions.

Just as the Pantheon had opened because of a demand for more theatre, so had the old Theatre Royal in Yeaman Shore. It was now called Breyer's or Yeaman Shore Theatre. That explains how Tom Powrie was able to make his stage début there. Another theatre, the Thistle Hall, had opened in Union Street to also meet the demand. This was a Regency style building (in the start of the Revival period) designed in 1833 by David Neave. It is now the "new" part of the Royal Hotel. Most of its façade has now gone -- except for the first story. But it is still an impressive building.

The Thistle Hall was run by a family named Gourlay. They produced what they billed as *Scottish Dramatic Scenes*, among other things. They also presented a version of *Othello*. He was played by an African known as Ira Aldridge. About that time, Ryder's leading man, Langley, took over. Under his management the Thistle Hall competed fiercely with the Theatre Royal. But it only lasted for a few weeks. The Theatre Royal survived. The Thistle Hall closed down.

As to Langley, he tried again. He redecorated and re-opened the Yeaman Shore building. While acting there his face was injured due to the discharge of a pistol. Another actor was cut by a sharp harpoon. These were like omens. Despite his opening with a strong stock company, it didn't pay. But soon after, when the Theatre Royal closed, he tried again there.

A production of a play on February 3rd 1846 looked promising. This was a local play, performed by the resident company, and about a local person -- Grizzel Jaffrey. She was the last witch burned in Dundee. The play was called *Grizzel Jamphrany* [Robertson]/*Jamphray* [Boyd], *the Last of the Witches* or *The Sea Captain of Dundee*. Ninety years later an adaption was the first radio play about Dundee. In the mid seventies, a version was staged in the Dudhope Arts Centre.

But by the late 1830s/early '40s "the theatre had gone out of fashion and both houses remained closed for over a year and right up to the half century it was a tale of disappointed actors and apathetic audiences."

About this time a new form of entertainment was becoming the rage. These were the Penny Gaffs -- so-called because of the admission price. They were the precursors of the Music Hall and were packed, noisy and in the kind of taste you'd expect for something so cheap. They ran several houses a night.

Scott of the Pantheon fame opened his gaff in the Meadows, in 1846, soon after the inferno. He called it the Royal Victoria Theatre. Everyone else in Dundee called it Wee Scotty's. And Scott filled it with actors from the recently closed other theatre in Yeaman Shore.

The most famous penny gaff was one in an upper floor if a hall in Lindsay Street. The proprietors called it the Clarence Theatre. The no-nonsense Dundonians called it Fizzy Gow's. McGonagall acted there to the mockery of the locals. He also spouted his doggerel in Wee Scotty's and in another gaff in the Seagate. But he wasn't the only one to go unappreciated by the Philistines! Scott's actors must have suffered a severe culture shock after performing at Breyer's -- which also went to the wall because of unappreciative audiences. And Willie Mc Kay -- another local actor reduced to performing in the gaffs -- ended his days doing an odd brand of busking: reciting Shakespeare to indifferent crowds in the Greenmarket.

Dundee's first music hall followed the Penny Gaffs. It was housed in the Exchange Building to the east of the Grassmarket (later Shore Terrace) at the foot of Castle Street; with Exchange and Dock streets either side. The building was built in 1828. It was better known as the Exchange Coffee House, frequented by the merchants, shipping agents and insurance brokers. Their offices were in Exchange Street. Soon after, it was refurbished and renamed the Dundee Music Hall. McGonagall played Hamlet, Othello and Macbeth there.

When its music hall days ended it became the City Assembly Rooms and then a masonic lodge. For several decades it was home to David Winter's -- printer, publisher, art supplier and stationer. The last time I was inside the building it was called *Le Bouquet Garni* (since closed down). By the 1950s the building still contained some relics of its music hall days. Etched on the glass panels of interior doors were harps and fiddles. And the original spring floor remained intact.

Meanwhile back up Castle Street the Theatre Royal went through further ups and downs till 1864. Then it was renovated and redecorated and had a new drop curtain painted by the scenery artist of the Bristol Theatre. The new manager, J.H. Robb of Edinburgh, employed a company of excellent players. The public at last responded and there was a run of successful plays.

After a short time of further alteration and improvement the theatre opened with *The Colleen Bawn*. This was a Victorian smash hit. House full notices were posted outside soon after admission times. It seemed the tide had turned for the Theatre Royal. The whole season was a sensation. Crowds packed the place to see *The Corsican Brothers, Workmen of Paris, Lady of the Lake* and *Octaroon*.

The good times rolled on for the Theatre Royal and two years later a new company played for a season and continued the successful run. It was managed by a Miss Heath who was to become famous at Drury Lane. She also married the equally famous actor Wilson Barrett.

The change about in the fortunes of the theatre may have been partly due to the Dundee theatrical magazine that appeared on the scene. The *Comet*, as it was called, was popular for twenty years. Quite an achievement, considering it was a theatrical magazine *and* for a town where theatre had not prospered. Granted, the *Comet* had been on the go for about two years before the successes in the theatre. But it must have had some affect on those successes.

On Monday, 24th February, 1869, Henry Irving played in the Theatre Royal.

That year the theatre's edifice was restored. During the following year the place closed for yet further "interior redecoration and extensive renovation." The old square side balconies where the weathiest patrons sat were demolished. The more modern horseshoe types replaced them. The wealthy patrons were to have a better view of the stage. Also, about a hundred and fifty individual stall seats were put in. These were now bookable. In fact, they were the only seats which were. Thus the term Box Office.

As Dundonians were spending more than ever on entertainment a circus opened opposite the East Station in Dock street -- at the foot of Allan Street (now East Marketgait). It soon became popular and was taken over by William MacFarland who had a knack for knowing what Dundee wanted entertainmentwise.

He renamed it the Alhambra Music Hall and the first notable venue there was billed as *McFarland's £600 Pantomime, Little Red Riding Hood.* It drew large audiences, further establishing the place as serious competition for the Theatre Royal. So did what Robertson called "...a new innovation styled *Hamilton's Diorama.*" Whatever that was, the Alhambra entered a period of rapid expansion. However, the police halted that by declaring the building as unsafe.

That would have pleased the Theatre Royal management. They excelled themselves in March of 1877 through booking the Carl Rosa Opera Company. On the afternoon of the 15th Dundonians saw the amazing cast of a hundred players. And they were conducted by Carl Rosa personally. Their programme for that week included *The Lily of Killarney, The Marriage of Figaro, Faust* and *La Traviata.*

It has to be said, though, that the management surpassed themselves because of McFarland. During the last ten years of the Theatre Royal's existence it prospered as never before. And under McFarland's management. He was a more than able manager. For a while he managed the Theatre Royal and Aberdeen's Her Majesty's Theatre simultaneously. He also managed the Music Hall in both cities.

Robertson tells us that in a "programme given for a Benefit Concert in 1884 there is an interesting item": THE PHONOGRAPH OR TALKING MACHINE.

So another Victorian diversion was on the way that would affect the size of theatre audiences. And they *were* soon being affected. It obviously had nothing to do with McFarland's management skills. The Theatre Royal had always been successful under his control. But even in spite of excellent performances, the theatre could not be saved.

As all good things come to an end so did the Theatre Royal's popularity. Though it became a music hall during its last year it was to no avail. The last thing they ever staged there was a typical Victorian melodrama called *The Life and Death of Jo.* It was an adaption from Dickens' *Bleak House.* Jenny Lee, who played the main character, rose from a touching deathbed scene to take a dozen enthusiastic curtain calls. She then made a tearful speech, followed by the band playing *God Save the Queen*, and the building's days as a theatre ended.

That happened on September 21st 1885. On the following 19th October Her Majesty's Theatre and Opera House opened in the Seagate, at the top west side of Gellatly Street. It literally took the city's breath away. (A review of Boyd's description in the foreword explains sufficiently.) Hardly surprising when the cost was £12,000. That was a phenomenal sum for the time and a good reason for the public being invited to participate in £10 shares.

The result of the shares surprised everyone. The required capital was oversubscribed and the theatre opened well in the black. Each year of its existence was one of successful runs. Certainly successful for a theatre by Dundee standards!

As its success was apparent from the outset, McFarland tried to make a go of the old Theatre Royal as a variety house. It had an auspicious start, causing him to have it renovated. But for once luck was against him. Even a benefit concert could not revive its fortunes. (Robertson gives the impression that it happened *after* the calamity below.) As in earlier times, the Freemasons came to the theatre's aid. The benefit concert was under the auspices of the Principal Grand Lodge of Forfarshire and the Board of Dundee Masonic Lodges. But the turn out at the benefit was high in spite of exorbitant prices, showing how highly he was esteemed by the locals.

The new show was billed to open on October 8th, 1888, but a fire gutted the place on the previous Saturday. McFarland, though, did not completely retire till 1891, after serving the theatre -- amateur and professional alike -- for quarter of a century. He'd lived for some years in Newport but moved down to Southport in Lancashire where he died in 1898.

Variety as we now know it came to Dundee in 1893 when a theatre opened behind the Queen's Hotel. Local historians tell us it was originally situated in Lochee Road, near to Dudhope Crescent Road. But *that* was the People's Palace. And it was run by Livermore who was in competition with Zeigler. Zeigler ran the one behind the Queen's Hotel. It was called the Royal Theatre Varieties. It burnt down and the building that replaced it was the Palace Theatre -- built by Livermore. It was a comparatively popular variety theatre into the 1970s. Scottish comedians such as Lex McLean, Jack Milroy, Ricky Fulton. and Johnnie Victory drew their fans there almost till it's closure.

From 1895 to 1905 was the peak period of theatrical activity in Dundee. The period of what Robertson calls "legitimate theatre" in Dundee. This was because every theatrical production promoter had to obtain a licence from the J.P. Court. In 1895 only one was granted. It went to Robert Arthur, lessee of Her Majesty's. Only one other licence was given in 1898 to a John Young for an unnamed theatre in Brown Street. The following year another was given to Arthur Henderson for his premises in Anderson's Lane, Lochee. By that time Young's theatre was called the Alhambra, to be renamed the Tivoli the next year. In 1903 a licence was given for the Empire in Rosebank Street.

The peak of the peak years was 1904 when two licences were given -- for the Gaiety (later the Vic) in Victoria Road and for the Comedy Club of Dundee to perform plays in the City Assembly Rooms. So that year Dundee had six theatres staging regular plays and a variety hall that had shows featuring Marie Lloyd, Harry Lauder, Will Fyffe and other Victorian and Edwardian Variety immortals.

With this rise in the fortunes of Dundee's theatre another local magazine was produced -- *What's On!* It reflected the sober thinking of the time and reviews were not given to houses they considered improper. But these were heady days for the theatre in Dundee. But they did not last long. A new invention was to put an end to all that -- the movie camera. Early in 1910 Dundee was to have it's first cinema. Known as the *Electric Theatre*, it was opened in the Nethergate, several yards from where the later Green's Playhouse was erected.

Dundee cinema, as Roberson wrote "...simply leapt into maturity. Dundonians forsook the theatres for these new cinemas so the decline in the former was as rapid as the rise of the latter." It seemed an unfortunate time for the King's to open a year before Dundee's first cinema! A time of the beginning of the end for Dundee theatre, including for the kind of variety for which the King's itself was opened.

Variety, as mentioned, continued into the seventies with the Palace Theatre. It was the only theatre to last that long. And neither it nor any other theatre in Dundee could play again to the kind of packed houses that the cinemas filled -- to the advent of TV. Though, after being renamed the Savoy in 1918, it closed to re-open in September 1924 as the Palace Cinema. It's first film was *Blood and Sand*, starring Rudolph Valentino. It reverted to a theatre in 1938 renamed, simply, The Palace. It was eventually called the Theatre Royal in 1968, closing three years later. It would occasionally re-open for amateur and professional shows. They were finally put to a halt because of a fire which swept through the building during the early morning of October 12th .

There was to be a revival of "serious" theatre though. The Dundee Rep got off the ground during the first winter of the Second World War. It appeared to be an odd time to start a theatre when, as Robertson noted, "People were uncertain, unused to new blackout restrictions, fearful against the day or night when all their horrid air raid precautions might be tried and found sadly wanting."

Yet, there was a desire for some people to escape the awful present and club together with like minds. Also, a floating population of the armed forces personnel were stationed in or near Dundee. Many were from England and had a tradition of theatre-going. So, filling a gap for them, the Rep had a successful beginning.

From their very beginning they were producing fine plays. The first, *Hassan* -- staged in December 1939 -- gave Richard Todd his break before he carved out a career in films. Many famous actors got their breaks there and already established actors have played in its three different locations. These include Arthur Lowe,

Virginia McKenna, Edward Fox, Michael York, Glenda Jackson, Nicol Williamson, Jill Gascoine, Tom Conti, Phyllis Logan and Joanna Lumley.

The original Rep was in Nicoll Street off Ward Road. The red sandstone building still stands. As seems to be a habit with Dundee theatres, it was gutted by a fire -- in June 1963. The company were homeless for several months before taking over the former Dudhope Church building in Lochee Road. That was less suitable for a theatre than the Foresters' building. But it was only intended for eighteen months use. It was the Rep's home for over eighteen years!

The new Rep in Tay Square opened with an inaugural performance on April 8th 1982. The Gala opening followed on May 4th.

Dundee theatre has had a turbulent history. As I said at the start, a cursory glance at our history would give the impression that we have a long-standing tradition of dramatic appreciation. In reality it was only a few who ever did. I reckon the above historical sketch clarifies it. And I don't think things have changed much.

Brian Cox, our most famous actor of the twentieth (and, so-far, the twenty-first!) century shows how far one Dundonian has gone in the world of drama. Dr Cox was from the Hilltown area and educated at St Michael's. He is not only famous nationally -- an amazing enough achievement -- but internationally. He is justifiably a celebrity of whom we can be proud.

When Gordon Burnside's play *A Man at Yir Back* was staged on the Rep it attracted Dundee people to the Rep who normally would never have set foot in a theatre. A good sign, I feel, that plays by local playwrights will draw the crowds.

Brilliant productions of classics in Dundonese have also been produced at the Rep. But most Dundonians are not interested in classics. That may just be why little seems to be written of regarding the Dundee theatre. Journalists can only write according to the tastes of their audiences. The public reaction to the theatre, sadly, has never been that encouraging.

Things will only get better theatrewise in Dundee when more people get involved to change our historical local attitudes. Apathy destroys. Activity builds. We can't have it both ways. Common sense, if not history, says so.

Robertson rightly tells us, "Dundee's problem has always been radically the same; not that of finding a theatre but that of maintaining an audience." That is why many theatres had to become cinemas. It is why we lost our greatest theatre, the King's.

But, in spite of the curious history of our theatre we can be optimistic about the future. Dundee has grown rapidly as a city with a population made up of people from "a' the airts". There is also a larger floating population of students and those in temporary and seconded employment than ever before. And people travel much further than in the past to visit Dundee. Some are from theatre-going backgrounds.

There is hope then. If we focus on what has been done and what can be done, even the King's could be resurrected.

THE KING'S, GODS AND COMMONERS

WHEN THE KING'S THEATRE opened on March 15th, 1909, it did two days after the *Dundee Advertiser* reported a rise in the city's crime rate. Up till the previous December 7758 crimes took place for that year -- an increase of 452 on the year prior to that. And a further 271 were put on probation. Drunkenness had only increased by three persons. Mind you, that put the number of drunks to 2835.

So, not only was the King's opened at an inauspicious time for Dundee theatre but also during a time of great social problems. One *Advertiser* headline attested to that. It stated, DUNDEE WOMAN SMOKER LIGHTS PIPE AND IS SEVERELY BURNED. The article concluded, "She is progressing favourably. She was taken to the infirmary in an ambulance van."

It reads today like deadpan comedy. Certainly *not* headline news. But pipe-smoking women weren't that uncommon among the poor while ambulance vans *were* fairly uncommon sights in Edwardian Dundee.

If the only upbeat thing worth reporting in the city was the opening of the King's, there is some cold comfort that the *Advertiser* had little or nothing upbeat to report form the larger world either. *It* had *it's* social problems too. Some equally as seemingly comic. Dundonians waiting and wondering what the opening day of the King's would herald could read the following statement in the *Advertiser*:

FOX AT HUNT DINNER

> Astonishment was caused at a dinner party at Lalow's hotel, Redhill ...The unexpected appearance of a fox which jumped through the coffee room window onto the table. Champagne bottles, glasses, flowers, vases, and plates were strewn in all directions... A waiter was rolled over in the melee... After racing around the room... the fox was cornered and bagged, but not before one or two in the extraordinary chase were bitten.

The same paper included another story under the headline FIGHT AT A BALL -- YOUNG BILBAO ARISTOCRATS ATTACK THE ORCHESTRA. The report goes on to tell of split heads, wrecked instruments and screaming ladies. And a short piece under the headline DUEL BETWEEN TWO OFFICERS mentioned that a naval lieutenant, Baron von Pegler returned home at an unexpected hour to find his wife, a well-known beauty, in the company of Chevalier de Resner. The result was the duel. There was also a report of a New York policeman, on holiday in Italy, being shot by a notorious Palermo gang called the Black Hand. And free speech in Russia was pretty much as usual. A magazine there was fined the equivalent of £50 and the editor of another to be prosecuted for publishing an article by Tolstoy.

That, then, was the world -- at least, as the *Dundee Advertiser* saw it -- on the opening day of the King's.

Dundonians had watched the building being constructed as a whole new central part of Dundee had developed. This development was a kind of evolution over a few decades. The population continued to rise at an alarming rate and the central area was grossly overcrowded, disease-ridden and half-ruinous. As there had been no town planning executed since 1839 it's not hard to imagine what the centre of Dundee looked like thirty years later. (Even then it was a great enhancement on what it was before the 1825 Bill for town improvements. The population had doubled by that time from fifty years earlier. Most dwellings were wooden slums, having changed little from medieval times.)

The housing problem actually became so severe that mill owners were forced to provide housing for their workers at their -- the mill owners' -- own expense.

William Mackison, who became Burgh Engineer and surveyor in 1868, tackled these problems with gusto. All plans for new buildings had to be submitted for his inspection. He was ever on the lookout for potentially offensive buildings. He altered plans frequently and ruthlessly and abridged anything he considered substandard. Between 1871 and 1891, he rebuilt the whole of the pre-Georgian part of the central area, except the Vault, the Overgate and parts of the High Street. Though Dundee saw great changes over those two decades, many buildings of exceptional architectural and historical interest were demolished in the process.

"Though the Improvement Act of 1871 was helpful," as Dr N.K. Subedi tells us in his *100 Years Town Planning in Dundee*, "it was carried out in the absence of a well thought out plan for the city as a whole."

The drastic clearance resulted in a great boon in tenement building. This was needed to rehouse those made homeless by the demolition. It was also needed because of the much increased population. Most of these lived in (what is now) the central area. The wealthier middle classes had been moving to the suburbs, Perth Road, Broughty Ferry Road and the Kingsway being the outer limits. Invergowrie -- indeed Ninewells -- and "the Ferry" were not considered Dundee at that time. And the Kingsway, not then constructed, was still virtual countryside.

The poorer people were being housed in the tenements. Some in the Cowgate and St Andrews Street, to the immediate east of the King's Theatre. As yet they had not been the beneficiaries of James Thomson's foresight. He was the City Architect and father of Frank Thomson, the King's architect. He, James, was appointed City Architect in 1904 and in 1906 (in succession to Mackison) also became City Engineer. He was a genius who, had his ideas been taken up by the City Fathers, would have transformed Dundee into an architectural showpiece of Britain, if not of Europe. His ideas -- as his drawings and plans show -- were as altruistic as they were aesthetic. He was appalled at the conditions in which the Dundee poor lived and set about trying to rectify their situation, as proposed in his Central Improvement Scheme of 1910.

Thomson had come to Dundee in 1872 to join the staff of Burgh Surveyor. He had contributed to many of the major developments, including the widening of Perth Road, the first tramways, the provision of electric and gas, cattle markets, slaughter houses, public baths and hospitals. But, as his hands were proverbially tied, the poorer classes remained confined to the dimly lit tenement slum areas of Watson Street, Blackscroft, Hilltown and Dens Road (among others) that were usually within walking distance of at least one jute mill.

These tenements were divided into many two- and sometimes one-roomed dwellings that often housed large families. Sanitation consisted of one cold-water tap per household. That luxury by no means extended to all tenants. Many Dundonians had to share a tap with a whole landing. Almost all tenement dwellers had to share outside lavatories. A visit to the King's would be a very special treat for those folk.

But just as it was not a good year for Dundee theatre it was also a particularly bad one for the Dundee building trade. The *Dundee Year Book* for 1909 tells us that "both contractors and workers have suffered -- the former in particular."

According to the *Dundee Advertiser* this was due to a large amount of Corporation work being undertaken by the Works Department itself rather than it being contracted. It was most certainly of benefit to the Works Department workers. It meant they had work. Of course, it also meant that those working for private companies were laid off. Though it cost the Corporation (and presumably the taxpayer) more the former's spokesmen claimed the recipients received a "better class of work." But public pressure caused the Council to pass a resolution that would "have the effect of curtailing the amount of work done by the men directly employed by the Corporation."

Surprisingly, it was reported in the *Dundee Year Book* that wages were maintained at the old rate despite the surplus labour in existence and "...this has had the effect of sustaining peaceful relations between employers and employed."

Most of the construction that year was in public buildings. These included the physics laboratory at University College, Dens Road School, the Drill Hall for the Territorials, two skating rinks (one in Dock Street and one off Blackness Avenue), a Pumping Station and Drainage Works in Downfield and the Electric Station at Stannergate and sub stations for the Electric Department were completed. A diphtheria pavilion was added to King's Cross Hospital and an extension was made to the Public Baths. Restoration work was done on the City Churches. And, by the end of the year, a start had been made on the construction of the Ward Road Public Library and Reading Rooms and on St Roque's District Library at Blackscroft. And the Technical College in Bell Street was still under construction.

Had it not been for those projects, the building trade would have been in a worse state. Indeed, it was so bad that the other constructions were "of the most unimportant character." These were jute warehouses, and building alterations. They included some cottages. But the building of housing for the poor almost ground to a halt. This was especially the case in the realm of the tenements. It was a worrying situation as the working-class population was growing at an alarming rate. Though things didn't seem too bad for the upper middle-class.

Things looked so bleak that the *Dundee Year Book* for 1909 stated, "It is to be regretted that the outlook for the coming year is anything but bright." And the *Dundee Year Book* for *that* year showed their outlook to be quite correct!

FRANK THOMSON'S BUILDING defied the times. It stood in stark contrast to the adjacent and facing tenements in the Cowgate: Most of the latter were typical coursed and snecked rubble buildings, made of local stone. (They stood till spring of 1973 when the Wellgate was demolished to prepare way for the Wellgate Centre.) The buildings to the immediate West of the King's, running into the Murraygate were similar. (The ones which now stand there were not erected until 1910.) The King's edifice was ashlar -- cut, shaped stone blocks of a dark red sandstone.

It has to be said, though, that this wasn't the first of the few sandstone buildings in the centre of Dundee. The *Courier* building (by the same firm of London architects, incidently, for whom Frank Thomson was working when he designed the King's), preceded it by about three years. A block of pleasant Victorian flats in the Nethergate, facing Miln's buildings, are of the same local sandstone. And those were built in 1890.

Frank Thomson himself chose the stone for the King's. We can but wonder if he conceived the idea through his firm's use of the medium in building the *Courier* building. Who knows? His firm may have inquired of him what was available locally prior to choosing stone for the *Courier* building, he being the

Dundonian on the staff. But I am only pondering here. None of the local historians or architects with whom I have discussed the matter have been able to tell me where exacty the sandstone came from.

However. It wasn't only the difference, size and colour of the stone that made the distinction. The design was also quite a contrast. As David M. Walker points out in his *Dundee Architecture & Architects 1770-1914*, "The St Andrew's Street elevation is strong, asymmetrical and dramatic."

Admittedly, he scarcely mentions the Cowgate elevation, merely commenting that "...a subsequent re-arrangement of the entrances has much damaged the design of the Cowgate front." But this may have been due to the fact that he found depressing the later decision to alter the front. Also, the point he was making was not on the King's *per se*. It was only alluded to in relation to the Thomsons. And he did state, "These are but a few examples. The same excellence is to be found throughout Edwardian times, for the level of accomplishment was high."

And the level of accomplishment for the King's front was also high. But Dr Walker's statement can be misleading for thosewho have no grasp of the subject in detail. (I speak from experience!) For example, none of the stonework had been demolished from when the building was first erected to when he wrote his paper in 1955. Indeed it is still intact. Only the original canopy has gone, along with the wrought iron balconettes which ran the length of the three windows above the canopy. Though the wrought iron balconette on the lower corner window remains. What *had* been changed was the ground floor of the building.

There had been a sub-let shop "with large basement saloons" on the East side. One of the windows was on St Andrews Street and another, of the same size and design, on the Cowgate. The shop was entered by a door on the corner. Because of the symmetry it made it central. To the immediate West of the shop was the original three-door entrance, the central door separated from the others by Tuscan columns. To the West of that was the King's Theatre booking office & shop which was joined to the Bodega, the theatre bar. The last part of the King's building was the doorway to the King's restaurant on the first storey. (The adjoining building, Caxton House, though of the same kind of sandstone, was not Thomson's design. It was built the following year.)

The wooden parts of the shop fronts and doors were of a similar design. This included a Chippendale-like pattern of the glazing bars in the upper parts of the shops and Bodega windows. The panel windows on the doors were similar but with lattice panel windows above them. These designs were more curved and *art nouvea* influenced rather than Chippendale. The business names in the panels above the booking office shop and the Bodega were gold embossed lettering -- the type normally used on Victorian and Edwardian playbills.

These shop fronts had changed drastically by the time Dr Walker wrote his paper. The box office and shop had been stripped out and the whole front demolished. This was to make way for an extension to the entrance floor and a change to the entrance itself. That doubled in width, making three doors either side of a broad, banded ashlar pillar (the original separation point between the entrance hall and the booking office/shop). These ran the length of a new canopy -- itself running the length of the second to seventh windows above; the original canopy and doors having run the length of the second to fourth windows. This may have meant an alteration to the stone on the lower part but only in the way of an additional couple of pillars. But it seems to me an exaggeration to say that that had much damaged the design of the Cowgate front. (Unless he meant the entrance front itself.) True, the Bodega had by then become Millet's Stores and the original front of that was torn down to be replaced with a more fashionable one. That undoubtedly affected the aesthetics of the *ground* floor but not front *per se*.

Besides, the extra doors were of the same design as the remaining originals and matched the double door of the corner shop. The above mentioned broad, banded ashlar pillar balanced in quite well as there is one either side of the corner door of the shop at the St Andrews Street/Cowgate end. These complemented a matching one separating the booking office from the Bodega and two either side of the upstairs restaurant entrance. (To my knowledge, these at the restaurant entrance were never covered other than with paint, as now.) They also complement, still, the southern end of the St Andrews Street elevation, the southern part (also banded).

Admittedly, the ground level of the King's had become a disaster area, compared to what was there previous to the changes in the 50s and 60s. But that also went for the adjoining buildings round to the Murraygate. The SCWS became the proprietors of the shop areas from the doorway of what is now the Continental Ballroom (the original King's Theatre restaurant) to the Murraygate corner. And they covered the stone portals and dividing pillars with black mirror as, like Millets (as it's now called), they did with the overhead business name panels. That, and the horizontal Art Deco-type sign rising from the centre of the canopy to the architrave, bearing the new name of the Gaumont, could also have made the front *appear* unrecognizable. It certainly would to architectural buffs like Dr Walker. They would be looking at it through a more aesthetic filter than most of us.

It would be interesting to know what Dr Walker would have thought of the last external alterations prior to the present ones made by Brannigan's.

Those really did draw ones eyes from the building proper. That was their purpose! The canopy front -- when County Bingo had taken over -- was in garish colours with lettering that clashed with the front *and* with themselves! The Tuscan columns and broad ashlar pillars underneath and, indeed, the whole area that had originally been the booking office, were covered with depressing vertical dark blue tiles. The lattice windows above the door had also been blocked out by these things. The effect was that of the interior of a none too salubrious public lavatory or of the shower room in a particularly seedy public baths. They were completely incongruous with the entrance of the fine Edwardian theatre. It is astonishing to think that anyone could not only create such ugliness but actually destroy something of historical and artistic value to do so. It is all the more astonishing in that it was done by people in the building trade.

The shop on the corner is now an extension of *Deja Vu*. When County Bingo was in charge of the building, the shop was an amusement "arcade" called Big Apple. It was as ugly on the outside as it was inside. The panels above and beneath the windows were covered with horizontal white tiles. The result was reminiscent of a derelict fishmonger's. It not only clashed with its own interior and the County Bingo entrance -- which was already clashing with the stone edifice -- it actually increased the desolate atmosphere of St Andrews Street. (As I write, I am looking at a picture of the scene which is depressing enough on photograph.) It drew one's eyes away from the rest of the building so that the viewer was almost forced to notice the unsightly and ignore the Edwardian refinement.

To judge by what was being erected in and around Dundee the late 1800s/early 1900s, the Victorian and Edwardian citizens would have been aghast at such senseless interference with a perfectly elegant entrance. I wonder what Dr Walker would have made of it. Brannigan's have to be congratulated for tearing down those awful tiles and opening again to public admiration the central and divider ashlar pillars and the Tuscan columns.

This tearing out of the false edifice shows that it was possible to return the whole front to its almost pre-late sixties' design (so-called). I daresay it would be possible, at some future date, if some wealthy restoration purist wanted to return it to the original Frank Thomson front, it could be done. The additional stone could be moved. What goes up can easily come down, especially as it wasn't holding up anything in the first place. This would apply to the two Tuscan columns erected in the 50s on widening of the entrance.

That could, of course, only be carried out if another booking office & shop were to be erected. And that isn't very likely. I'm simply allowing myself to dream out loud here because, though improbable, it's not an impossible project. But to turn it into a reproduction of the original would require taking over Millets and reverting the Bodega and also getting contol over the upstairs Continental Ballroom. We're talking a lottery-winning restoration purist here.

And then there is the argument that it would simply be a museum piece as it's not very likely, in this day of so many alternative choices of audiovisual entertainment, that a theatre could draw crowds enough to warrant a booking office, restaurant and bar for them. Though I can't see what's so bad about it becoming a museum piece. It would still be preferable to the present state of things.

So, back to reality...

THE FIRST DAY the King's opened, it received the public acclaim it deserved. The opening itself was vitually celebrated. And by Dundonians of all classes. For those among the poorer classes who lived across the street in the squalid tenements, it was a special day; one they would remember for a long time.

It was a treat for the poor just to look at the rich and powerful who attended the opening ceremony. In those days there were class barriers between labourers/ millworkers and tradesmen, and between tradesmen and department store assistants. Office clerks were considered a cut above all of these. The inhabitants of the North side of the Cowgate, like those in the eastern part, would have been on the bottom rung of the ladder of Dundee society. They would have considered office workers as well above their station. Architects and other officials, in their minds, would have been on a par with the superstars of today.

The buildings on the North side -- where the Wellgate Centre now stands -- were the front to Bain Square and to the back court of an attached tenement. The Bain Square front ran from the Style & Mantle shop at the Wellgate corner to a bank which was, roughly, opposite the King's booking office (to the immediate West of the entrance). The attached tenement -- the front of which was fifteen to sixteen yards or so back from edifice of the Bain Square front -- was adjoined to the wall of the St Andrew's church graveyard. Its ground floor had a central close entrance with, latterly, a carpet shop to the West side and a savings bank to the other. Bain Square was entered by a pend (level-vaulted archway) from both the Cowgate and Wellgate.

The crowds swarming in the street hoping to catch a glimpse of the Edwardian celebrities -- Lord and Lady Dunedin -- applauded them warmly when they finally arrived in their chauffeur-driven limousine. The baron and his wife were attending the laying of the foundation stone ceremony in the vestibule, the latter performing the honours. The stone sealed a bottle of coins of the realm and some contemporary newspapers. It can still be seen above the interior entrance of *Deja Vu*'s.

The architect Frank Thomson, accompanied by his brother, presented her ladyship with a silver trowel. She also received an ivory mallet, a gift from the builders. Then, according to the following morning's *Dundee Advertiser*, the stone "was then declared well and truly laid."

After the stone-laying ceremony James Lockhart presented her with a silver standard lamp. He was a representative of Maxwell, Son & Co., the Dundee electrical suppliers and fitters of the King's lighting. We are informed of this via the *Advertiser*, which also stated that "through this lamp she switched on the whole of the electric light in the theatre."

That was the cue for the party to proceed to the stage.

As soon as they entered the auditorium they were applauded by an audience that had filled every seat. After almost a century's hindsight, it can seem quaint that enough people to pack a theatre would turn up for a mere opening. But we have to consider the times. To see a theatre suddenly streaming with electric light was not an everyday occurrence -- especially when the streets and vast majority of houses were lit by dim gas mantles. That includes the homes of the wealthy. Many dwellers of the tenements had to make do with paraffin or candles. So it was quite an event for the audience. And it would have been for many future ones.

There were a number of others who accompanied Lord and Lady Dunedin to the platform. These were all local dignitaries, including a former Lord Provost. Their Chairman introduced Lady Dunedin, stating that it was her first visit to Dundee and that if she again "favoured them with her presence she would receive as hearty a reception." The audience applauded in assent.

On taking the floor she said that it was fortunate for them "...the days are past when acting is considered a vice and actors regarded as disreputable people. People now realize the importance of drama, not only as an amusement but as an education.

"What better education can be got than by witnessing the works of Shakespeare, who had such a marvellous insight into human nature, and such marvellous power of portraying it?

"Scotland is, perhaps, somewhat slow in waking up to the value of drama. But Scotsmen never make up their minds rashly or hurriedly. They always carefully deliberate until they are fully convinced. And then, having formed an opinion, they stick to it."

She further buttered up the audience by saying that a celebrated London actor had recently told her that actors like to go to Scotland "because Scottish audiences are so sympathetically intelligent."

The baroness had a sense of humour. No doubt, she suggested, they had all heard the story of the sarcastic Englishman who said it took a surgical operation to make a Scotsman see a joke. " 'Yes,' answered the Scotsman, 'An English joke, because there is no point in it.' "

The audience replied with laughter.

"If a Scottish audience is moved to laughter over a joke, you may be sure it is a good one. And if it is moved to tears or emotion over a tragedy or pathos you can be sure the subject is worthy of emotion."

She then mentioned that not only education but religion played a part in the Greek drama but that it would always be foreign to our (presumably Scottish) nature to have religious subjects or scenes from Scripture "brought before us" on stage. She did concede, however, that Continental religious plays were "most solemn and impressive and produced a real religious effect."

Her talk then focused on the acting profession:

"We often hear people speak as if those who went on stage did so to amuse themselves. But that is a great mistake and actors and actresses are about some of the hardest working people I know. Behind the glamour of the footlights is a great deal of drudgery and hard work.

"Nothing is harder than to make jokes when one is out of spirits and depressed." After saying so she then made the following statement, presumably to illustrate the point:

"You have all heard the story of Grimaldi who, when he was run down, consulted a doctor. The doctor did not recognize him and said, 'All you want is a hearty laugh. Go and see Grimaldi.' "

The audience laughed, apparently as much as at her first joke. Either Dundee humour has changed much or the audience were being polite.

Lady Dunedin herself concluded on a polite note. She wished every success to the "beautiful house and the flourishing city it adorns."

She was heartily applauded. Then one of the dignitaries presented her with a bouquet of flowers. And after Mr Alfred Moul, Chairman and Managing Director of the Company, proposed a vote of thanks to Lady Dunedin.

After more applause Lord Dunedin then took the floor. He thanked the audience for their kind reception of his wife's stage debut. They laughed in reply. He wondered, he said, if the Chairman saw the dilemma in which he had put him:

"For if I make a long and eloquent speech it would be a little hard on my wife. While if I bore you -- which is much more likely -- however good it might be for my humility to know I cannot speak as well as my wife, in view of the public position I hold, I don't know if that fact should be rubbed into me."

That was received with as much laughter as his wife's jokes.

"No doubt there is a great amount of curlers in the audience. And they would know that the skip sometimes has great things to do. But there are also times when the less he does is better. As an experienced curler, I know when to hogg."

It was greeted with further laughter and applause.

As the audience made its way outdoors the theatre's orchestra, conducted by Ernest G. Summerfield, the musical director, "provided an excellent selection of music."

As the commoners filtered through the King's exits, the aristocrats and the dignitaries headed for the Royal Hotel in the Nethergate. There a luncheon was held and after "loyal and patriotic" toasts were proposed and replied to, Lord Dunedin gave a longer one to the Corporation of Dundee. This was, he said, because it was the Lord Provost and Magistrates and Chief Constable who gave him his first leg up in his professional career."

That and more irrelevant details about the luncheon filled columns of the following day's *Advertiser.*

More was written on the Dunedins' speeches in the King's, and on Lord Dunedin's toast in the Royal Hotel and on what was said by whom and to whom there, than the report on the King's first night and the other four theatre reports put together. The above Advertiser quote was the most interesting and entertaining of the whole report. But it is worth mentioning the report as it shows the difference between social concepts and attitudes of then and now as it does the things considered significant and newsworthy.

When the lights went on to welcome the audience of the King's first theatre production, the reaction must have been the same as that of the audience at the opening -- one of surprise and delight and further surpise and delight as they took in the surrounding interior. The low lights would have given people access to their seats, then once they were settled the rest of the lighting would have been turned on. I can't imagine the audience having just fumbled around for their seats in the darkness and to sit there till Lady Dunedin switched the lights on!

I can, however, imagine their anticipation for the appearing surroundings -- whetted two days previous by the Advertiser report: "...whether for skilful arrangement, sumptuousness of furnishings, or in the comfort which it will afford to its patrons, the new house will take a high place amongst provincial theatres."

No-one could have been disappointed. I frequented the place as a child and never ceased to be fascinated by the interior. I still have vivid memories of my reactions when the main lights came on after a film. I was around 12- or 13-years old when the place was "renovated" and my sense of disappointment for the changes was revived each time I returned to see a film. So it's easy for me to imagine the awe and delight an Edwardian Dundonian would experience on his/her first visit.

The sheer grandeur of the place raised the enthusiasts' eyes upwards. The urge to do so was aided and abetted by the pilasters on the box walls. These led the eye up to the arches above each of the two upper boxes; both had a Baroque head and other ornament on the moulding. Each of these two mouldings -- facing each other across the auditorium -- were in a corniced blind archway that led the eye to the ceiling. So did the proscenium and the spandrels -- to which its two long marble columns either side guided the eye. These were a variegated pink and rouge marble.

As your eyes met the ceiling, you couldn't help but let them follow the circling, elaborate, moulded cornicing. The moulding, whatever and wherever it was, led the eye to another part -- but was exquisite to the point where it made it want to return, if not remain. It all gave the impression of flowing exuberance -- including the balcony fronts which bevelled outwards either end and swept inwards to a central bend -- as is the wont of Baroque-style interiors. In fact, some of it bordered on Rococo (such as the heads atop the arches of the upper boxes), especially as it was light in colour, as opposed to the dark and heavy Baroque.

For me, it was the kind of theatre that, wherever I sat, whenever I was inside, I wanted to be somewhere else to experience the view from there. Prior to a film (I never did see a stage production there), or during an intermission, I'd look around and choose my imagined seat. But it was a common thing to see people admire the surroundings when the lights were on. (Perhaps they too were imagining themselves in other seats.) The photograph of the interior from the stage (see below) view will show why.

As it was such a spectacular place, it's difficult to know where to begin in describing it.

But it's fair to say that the "real" commoners sat in the "gods"! Being one of them, I usually did. Because they were the cheapest seats. The gods, less colloquially, were the gallery or upper circle. The highest balcony, if you like. It was also the steepest. The tops of the seat backs were virtually in line with where the feet were of the people behind. It meant that every member of the audience had a clear view of the stage.

This was most unusual for a gallery. Being the cheapest seats, these in most theatres were the places where the audience had the worst view. Frank Thomson, like his father before him, had concern for the poorest recipients of his clients' demands.

It was such a high gallery that the balcony front was in line with the entablature of the blind arches (on the box walls) and the architrave of the proscenium. So, those in the front and lowest row were still at a vantage point of at least thirty feet above the stage.

The *Dundee Advertiser*'s reporter of the time claimed that the dome was sixty feet above the the stalls. Judging from the print in the *Dundee Year Book* of 1909, the front of the gods and the top of the proscenium are roughly halfway in height between the stalls and the dome centre, if not a few feet higher. The people in the gods had an excellent view of the dome. But I have to digress here to make some points regarding this "dome."

The picture in the *Dundee Year Book* shows only less than half of the ceiling. It is difficult to discern from it whether the ceiling is round or oval -- though the impression it gives is oval. It was often referred to, originally, as the oval ceiling. Till recent times it could be seen through a false ceiling. (And while the present false ceiling blocks out any view of the dome, it is still preserved above it.) I was given some pictures of it taken soon after Brannigan's were proprietors of the building. If it was domed it isn't noticeably so in these pictures. The ceiling looks quite level on all but one. I do recall it being very slightly domed but I was only twelve or thirteen when I last saw it -- nearly forty years ago. And my memory is not the best. But the other aforementioned photo gives the impression of slight curvature. And yet another picture I've been given, taken from inside the roof, shows the upper part to appear slightly domed. But not nearly so as the impression given in the *Dundee Year Book*.

There is an extant photograph (mentioned above) once sold as a postcard (see photograph A), that shows it as quite domed also. It also shows it as oval. Though the one in the *Dundee Year Book* is an artist's impression -- a clearer version of the one that appeared in the *Dundee Advertiser* of the Saturday before the opening day -- the artist evidently drew it from "life." That would seem obvious from other details he's depicted. Unless his impression was taken from a
photograph. But though it has been bromide screened for press -- as the dots show -- it is not likely a photograph itself. The angles of the box walls show this. The left side of the upper circle show this also. Unless, again, it was a particularly faded photo. Early photographs often were and had to be "touched up" by artists. That would explain the curvature of the dome if it were a photo.

It would also explain another point: The artist has depicted the ceiling as painted with naked classical-looking characters whose arms seem to be reaching up to the ring of a cornice that their heads touch. They don't appear to be angels as they have no wings. There are other sketchy scenes between these larger characters. Though the whole ceiling isn't depicted, if the symmetry is correct there's enough room for eight to ten of these characters/angels.

The postcard/photograph also shows a painted ceiling with semi-naked angels with outstretched arms. Only two can be seen. But, if we are expected to assume that the symmetry on that is also consistent, there would be room for at least six, possibly eight angels. But what can be discerned from this photo is that there can be no more than four angels, if they were all the same style. The outstretched arms of the others would be apparent otherwise. The only impression one can get logically, then, is of four angels, two to the North side and two to the South -- with two large scenes (none of the ones here, either, are identifiable) between them on the East and West sides and two smaller scenes between them on the North and South.

Bill Dow, an expert on the work of the Thomsons, said he thought it probable that a special lens could have purposefully distorted the perspective. A point I take because it is obvious the ceiling isn't in perspective. That's apparent from the differing angle of the central light piece. Mr Dow also felt it was possible that the ceiling had been painted in on the photo. Because the ceiling is undoubtedly portrayed on it as oval and protruding into the ceiling above the gods.

I told him I was fairly certain, from memory, that one looked out from the gods to a round ceiling -- the round ceiling which is preserved above the present false one. And again, I'm only relying on memory here but I think the outer edge of the round ceiling cornice did not go into the ceiling space above the gods.

The angels on that ceiling are also as I remember them: high relief -- almost three dimensional -- plaster carvings or mouldings. They are certainly not paintings! These sculptures are also Art Deco in design. If one of the ceilings on either the yearbook artist's illustration or the one in the photograph is correct, then the preserved one is a later addition. As the theatre was closed for a period during 1928-29 for alterations, it may have been then the relief angels were added. That date would explain their Art Deco style. This was also when Art Deco was beginning to make an impact in theatres and cinemas in Britain.

But Stephen Fraser could not find anything in his extensive researches pointing to this having occurred. The architect's daughters, Gertie and Trixie Thomson, do not believe the ceiling was changed at that time. I hasten to add that what these ladies don't know about their father's work is hardly worth knowing! Of course, it isn't likely that a whole ceiling would be changed.

It's interesting to note, though, that in the artist's impression, and in the photograph, the nudes'/angels' feet appear to be resting on cabachon-like moulded settings in the cornice. The sculptured angels' feet are resting on similar "cabachons."

I am still in two minds regarding these sculpted angels being original. Not having the facts, I don't know whether it would have been possible to add them at a later date. But I feel they are too in-your-face to belong to the Edwardian period.

The bare breasts were surely *de trop* for Presbyterian Scotland only eight years after Queen Victoria's death. And there's another point to be considered:

A *Dundee Advertiser* reporter wrote, "But the chef d'oeuvre of internal embellishment is the treatment of the dome... Its great expanse is filled with allegorical paintings -- bold in outline, warm in colour, and effective in the extreme. Above the proscenium the curving front is similarly decorated. This work is by F. De Jong of London."

So we can be certain that the dome was filled with paintings. We even have the artist's name. But even if the paintings were painted over in 1928-29, there is no mention in the above *Advertiser* report of carved or moulded angels. It can hardly be argued that the writer ignored them because of the prudishness of the times. If that was the case, the architect wouldn't have designed them nor the sculptor/plasterer made them. Furthermore, the artist's drawing and "touched up" photograph could easily be shown to be in error if the present angels were there.

Yet, it's not impossible for them to have been part of the original ceiling. Supposing they weren't painted in the colours they now are -- if they didn't have the wings they do -- they could pass for *Art nouveau*. *Art nouveau* can blend well with Baroque and Rococo. And Thomson did design art nouveau windows for the King's. *Art nouveau* was a style of that period.

It may well be that as a perceptive and ingenious designer he anticipated Art Deco before its time and thus the wings. One other thing is that these angels make a definite cruciform pattern. (Neither those in the artist's impression or the photograph do.) While it could be said that this hints at Frank Thomson's attention to symmetry, it doesn't really in the sense that they clash with the rest of his design. In my opinion, for what it's worth, they're almost too powerful and lack the refinement of Frank Thomson's work. Anyway, a future designer would have been well aware of the ubiquitous symmetry throughout the theatre's design. And it wouldn't then be likely for him to attempt anything that would upset the equilibrium. Especially so when introducing something as powerful as (virtual) three dimensional sculpture which will, to an extent, clash. Paintings of angels wouldn't do that -- as seen in both the artist's impression and photograph. At least, not if they were painted with the kind of refinement as these representations show.

As to what can be decided regarding this mystery of the ceiling, I leave that to you.

One thing that isn't possible at present is to figure out if the cornice did or didn't overlap into the space above the gods. The main floor of *Deja Vu*, built over the original stalls floor, has a new false ceiling. Unlike the one County Bingo had, it completely blocks out the dome. It should be easy to figure out on restoration.

Shona Duncan, the Assistant Manageress, showed me as much of the closed off upper theatre as was possible. There was no access to the gods -- the only other way we could hope to solve that particular mystery. Unless, of course, any reader has information to the contrary. The trust would appreciate any personal recollections or photographs that can help. They nor I have come to a decision on the matter. The plot thickens because I have in my possession a photo taken from the gods that seems to show a part of the cornice being above part of the gods

Returning from the digression, we're still in the gods. As the photograph shows, these were benches -- further explaining why they were the cheapest seats. The lower walls either side of the balcony wings were plaster. They had classical valanced mouldings running the length of the ceiling cornice. If there was original seating at those walls, it could only have been a single bench. It appearsin the photograph that this is as far as the outer part of the dome's cornice could have reached -- i.e., in line with where the furthest point of the valanced moulding penetrated into the gods. (This may account for an illusion of the cornice appearing to penetrate into space above the gods in the photo mentioned in the last paragraph.) The walls of the gods proper were wood panelling. Nothing fancy, as expected for the cheapest seats. But there was a view of everything else that was most fancy!

The walls of the dress circle were more elegant. These were large panels, in dark red, with white moulded framing. From one either side near the front there hung a wall lamp. Between them were pendant-like floriate classical moulding. Above them, the length of the walls climbing to the North side, was similar valanced mouldings to that of the gods, but not so long or wide.

There was similar panelling in the rear stalls or "pit" but without any of the mouldings. Being the cheapest seats next to the gods, what can you expect?

The people in the upper circle, the dress circle, the lower circle, and some in the back few seats of the stalls, had an excellent view of the stage, proscenium and the walls of the boxes either side.

These walls came out at a small angle tapering in slightly towards the stage. (The angles are exaggerated in the artist's impression. Mr Dow told me he reckoned that those in the postcard/photograph could be slightly tilted further than they actually were. He suggested that this too may have been due to a special lens used for that purpose.) They were absolutely delightful works of craftsmanship, reflecting Thomson's love of symmetry.

The boxes were the centrepiece. The upper one, from the top of its balcony to the ends of its arch, was the height of the dress circle balcony top to that of the upper circle (gods); the lower box approximately half of that. Each arch with the

Baroque head, as mentioned, on the upper box was a basket (or elliptical) arch as was the encasing blind arch. The basket arch was repeated above the entrance and exit either side of the lower box. These ideally reflected the cornice framing of De Jong's painting above the proscenium as it was also a basket arch. And the boxes and doorways either side were draped with crimson, velvet curtain. The curtains of the upper box and doorways were topped with drape pelmets of the same material. The ones above the doorways were gold fringed. (See picture A.)

The pilasters flanking each upper box and the panel either side had composite capitals holding up the Baroque style moulding to the arch. It, in turn, had the effect of a double capital. The lower pilasters flanking each lower box and the doorways either side had ionic capitals. Atop each was a kind of plinth-cum-corbel, including at either side of the lower balcony, of which it was the same height. This also had the effect of a double capital. The friezes either side, above the archways, and the ones beneath them and over the archways, made a kind of double entablature. (Picture A.)

The moulding on the balcony of each lower box was balustrading held up by a fanned acanthus leaf corbel. Salient points on the moulding -- e.g., fluting and bordering -- were highlighted in gold. The pendulum-like Renaissance designs on the panels either side of the upper boxes, the lettering above the doorways and the inner borders of the spandrels were lined also in gold.

Let alone the craftsmanship and the drama of it all, the symmetry itself was a work of art. Even the seating was symmetrical. That of upper circle and the whole of the lower auditorium were divided by a central aisle and aisles running the length of their walls. These, of course were stepped in the upper circle. The dress circle had two stepped aisles tapering inwards towards the balcony. It created three trapezoids in the seating arrangement, the centre one inverted. From the stage, the whole thing looked perfectly balanced. So the performers could enjoy Thomson's symmetry as much as the audience -- whenever they had the time to take it in!

Imagine, if you will, the curtain going up in those surroundings on the first show. Perhaps you can imagine the atmosphere too. It's not too difficult. At least it wouldn't be if it was similar to the usual crowds that attended shows in the King's.

The dress circle seats were considered the best and those who could afford them sat there. These were the upper eschelons of Dundee society. In those days when class was more clearly defineable than now, they would have had the "breeding", background and connections to go with their wealth. They would have dressed accordingly, the men in white tie and tails and the ladies in ball gowns.

Perhaps, occasionally, members of the aristocracy would have sat there. Though it was a dirtier town, with slums everywhere and mill chimneys spuming filth into the air, the upper classes from the surrounding counties visited the city fairly often then. In comparison to now, that is, as they were normally in residence only during the summer months.

Those among the well-off who wanted "to be seen" would try their best to get seats in the dress circle. Even if they weren't well-connected, there was kudos in those days being noticed in the quarters of the aristocracy -- albeit in a part of a theatre they only sometimes visited! Being seen there would at least give the appearance of being well-connected. There was an element of fashion connected with it too.The fact that the lower gallery was called the dress circle tells us something -- i.e., the patrons dressed for attendance.

These were also the most comfy seats. Fewer people were admitted into that area than anywhere else -- except for the boxes! They held about a third of any other area. So there was some justification for them being the most expensive seats. As the area held less, the theatre had to be compensated by charging double the price of the (front of the) upper circle.

But those who were well-off enough to have the next best seats would sit in the stalls. They wouldn't see themselves as being as common as those who were literally behind them in the lower pit. But they probably still "knew their place" in comparison to those in the dress circle. The stalls crowd, though, would still have been regarded as a cut above the majority of Dundonians -- bearing in mind the divisions I mentioned above among the working-classes. There would also have been very wealthy people sitting in the boxes, the upper ones being the most expensive.

Interestingly, the *Dundee Year Book* artist's impression shows a door leading from the dress circle into the upper box. This infers there was one either side. However, on the photograph this is not so. There are no doors but, instead, panels matching the others on the surrounding walls. Each has a radiator in the alcove beneath. This could mean that the panels and radiators were put in at a later date to cover up the doors. It would mean that the photograph would not be from 1910, as I'd been informed, but taken at a later date. As the theatre was converted in 1928-29, perhaps it was taken around that time.

It is known that when the building was turned into a cinema the amplifiers were placed in the upper boxes. As they would no longer have been used, it certainly would have been an opportune time to board up the entrances and install radiators. The arched doorways to the North of the lower boxes led into *them* as the doorways nearer the stage led respectively to St Andrews Street and the parallel back lane. It isn't too unlikely that the entrances could have also led to the upper boxes too. These would have been a quick way of getting out of the cinema via the doorways next to the stage. Also it would have been a quick way for the holders of the lower boxes to get to the bar and restaurant to the left of the upper circle during intermissions. Otherwise they would have had to pass the people in the pit.

The pit was on the same level as the stalls. It was behind them and usually these were fitted with wooden benches. While those in the stalls would be happy to have the rich and powerful in the boxes either side of them, they would not be too happy having the hoi polloi behind them. That's why they normally had separate exits and wooden barriers dividing them. Actually, photo A shows there are panels with alcoves underneath them, at either side of where the stalls ended and pit began. These alcoves are certainly where doors once stood. There is an outline showing where (I am told by one theatre historian) concrete coloured to look like sandstone had been inserted at a later date from the original on St Andrews Street and another in brick on the wall in the back alley. These are evidence that the panels above the alcoves cover original doorways. I have two other photos in my possession showing that there was a door on the St Andrews Street side, about halfway down the building. The panels and alcoves on photo A also show that it must have been taken much later than 1910.

Anyway. Because there was only five or six feet of headroom, and little space for air to circulate, the pits were normally hot, stuffy dark and smelly places. Nor would it have helped that people smoked in the theatres then. Except for the back of the gods these were the cheapest seats.

Even so, the people who could afford them would not have been scruffy riff-raff. Though perhaps they were in the eyes of those in the stalls. On some occasions *they* would be dressed in evening clothes. But those in the pits would be dressed in suits and dresses. Working people had their "Sunday best" in those days, which they wore going to the theatre. Well into the sixties working-class men and women dressed in suits and dresses at the weekends to go to dance halls and the cinema. So an evening at the King's would have warranted the same.

The prices were as follows: Dress circle 5/-, stalls 4/-, upper circle (gods) 2/6d, pit 1/- and back of the upper circle 6d. The boxes were a guinea and a half for four people. These were average prices for the time. They were probably fairly expensive for the poorer people but it wasn't a time of inflation. So, for the middle classes they were good prices.

And in one sense, though, there were no best views. The pillarless auditorium assured everyone of getting a clear view. Even those in the back part of the gods. After all, the view was normally included in the price of theatre seats. But not necessarily so with the King's -- another point that made it unique.

The idea was based on an American one from the turn of the century where the balconies are cantilevered. In other words, they're supported by a downward force behind a fulcrum -- the beams and girders behind the surrounding walls. So they are without external bracing and seem to be self-supporting. Frank Thomson applied this technique with the use of reinforced concrete. It was not only very clever but it provided satisfactory viewing for all.

That must have satisfied Frank Thomson because another speciality of his -- included in other theatres he designed -- was staggered seating. This design assured each audience member of being spared looking into the back of someone's head. And the head one was directly behind would have been sufficiently low not to block one's view.

So there was nearly all the stratum of Dundee society -- and some from farther afield -- from the richest to the better off working- (or lower middle) class antici- pating the King's Theatre and Hippodrome's first show of the Twentieth Century.

And what a show it was. Here's how the *Advertiser* put it under their headline of THE FIRST NIGHT AT THE KING'S:

> The first night at the King's Theatre proved to be a great success. At the first house the large audience was agreeably surprised at the magnificence of the interior of the building when the lights were turned on, and round after round of applause was indulged in. A really first-class entertainment was provided, and showed that the lessees are determined to maintain a high standard. In the course of the proceedings Mr Alfred Moul, the Managing Director of the United County Theatres, Ltd., the lessees, addressed a few words to the audience, complimenting the promoters of the Company which had erected the theatre on the magnificence of the buil- ding, and declaring that it was one of the handsomest he had seen in the country. His company promised to endeavour to bring the best of talent to it, and to spare no expense to make it the success it deserved to be. After the company had appropriately opened the proceedings by singing the National Anthem, the programme was entered upon, and notwith- standing that it was a first night, and everything was new, there was not a hitch. An attractive and picturesque turn was that of Sidy Nirvanah and her posing white horse; and Wallau, a juggler, who followed, introduced several novel and particularly clever tricks. An attractive and exciting im- personation of Parisian life -- "A Daughter of Pleasure" -- was cleverly presented by Grahame and Harrington. The most popular item was that provided for by the Four Royal Scots -- ladies of Scotch extraction. All that they did savoured of the land of cakes, and even of the Highlands, for

one of them sang very sweetly a Gaelic melody. As singers they were very successful, while as dancers and manipulators of various kinds of instruments they commanded well deserved applause. Bransby Williams, possessed of rare elocutionary powers, gave selections from the works of Charles Dickens. Though most of them were from "David Copperfield," including such characters as Micawber and Uriah Heap [sic], he essayed the farewell speech of Sydney Carton in the "Tale of Two Cities," and here he was particularly true to the character and rendered the speech with great power. A humorous play, "Jack and the Giant Killer," was provided by George Auger and Co.; Victor and Louis, as comedians, created much merriment; and Hamilton Hill, an Australian baritone, made a favourable impression.

And I can imagine those impressionable folk making their respective ways home. So much for today's gap bewteen rich and poor being wider. Then there were almost unsurmountable gaps between the rich and the very rich, the comfortable and the not-so-comfortable and, as mentioned already, between the poor and the really poor. And in those days these things also related to their educational status.

The aristocracy and the really wealthy, like jute mill-owning families, would have had their own drivers to take them home in their carriages. (Some of the mews flats of those drivers, with their stables -- now garages -- beneath, still stand in the older Dundee suburbs. There are several in the Broughty Ferry area.)

The less wealthy, would have had their own carriages, but without their drivers. For there was a comfortable middle class in Dundee, wealthy enough to own carriages but not afford drivers. These were the professional classes who inhabited the terraced houses in the West End, such as those between West Park Road and Blackness Avenue. Though some of them did have their own drivers. Buildings in that area still contain their mews flats, long since converted to other uses.

Those who lived in the lower middle-class tenements of Blackness Avenue and thereabouts, would have caught a hansom cab at the ranks at Albert Square. If any of the less wealthy sitting in the pit or the gods lived out the West End they would have caught the tram. At that time one went out to a terminus near the Ninewells. Of course, many would have gone out Broughty Ferry way too, that being the other main suburb.

Perhaps the people of Bain Square looked from their windows with envy and/or admiration as they watched them leave the King's. The theatregoers perhaps wondered what had gone on in the other theatres. If so, they would relish reading the reviews the following morning in the *Advertiser*.

The Bondman, the play based on Hal Caine's novel, that opened at Her Majesty's. The Gaiety Theatre in Victoria Road certainly gave people variety. Flora

51

Cromer did impersonations there prior to a turn on a horizontal bar and rope. Next "Male Marie Lloyd" Montague Biggs performed a saucy act before Charles Sanatoni's soprano renditions. Ted Saunders did take-offs of stars of the day. Then Rose D'Aulby (an "ideal choral vocalist") sang, followed by George Grenville. He was apparently so famous for whatever it was he did that the critic didn't have to mention it! The last live act was Yellini, a comic juggler. The theatre closed after "a series of new pictures were displayed on the screen in electromotorscope."

The Empire Theatre at 62 Rosebank Street showed the *Merchant of Venice, A Sister's Love* and a "fine selection of comic films." The Cedrics in their comedy act, *Chish and Fips*, and Veda, a tightrope walker "Made a great hit in his *Tramp on the Wire.*" Whether these last acts were films or live theatre is difficult to say. The *Advertiser* review is a bit ambiguous to a modern reader. It was written for Edwardians, well aquainted with these performers. Live acts were often advertised under a title -- as you'll see in the next paragraph. And though a comedy act and a tightrope walker may not seem to us like the stuff of silent movies, neither does *The Merchant of Venice*! Though, in the review, it's obvious enough that it was just that. And -- I hasten to add -- this Empire was not the cinema with the same name, also in Rosebank Street. *That* was number 70. And it didn't open open till 1920, five years after the theatre closed.

The Palace Theatre's chief portion of entertainment that night was also the "pictures". Several were shown. The two which were most enjoyed by the audience were *A Week's Winter Sport in Savoy* and *Oliver Cromwell*. The films were followed by "a number of sparkling varieties, including Oliver Martyn in his comedy turn, *The Boxing Contest*. And Walker and May received great applause for their selection of "Coon and Darkie" songs.

So that was entertainment elsewhere the first night of the King's.

But what mustn't be overlooked is Frank Thomson's concern for the players. Their dressing rooms were built up in the flies, above the stage, giving them quick and easy access by a back stairway down to the stage. This was a most unusual arrangement. The windows of the dressing rooms -- four storeys -- can still be seen from St Andrews Street and the opening leading into the back alleyway.

For its time this was the height of luxury for the performers. And it did not go unappreciated. Frank's daughter, Trixie, gave me a copy of a letter she received in 1954 from Bransby Williams. He was the aforementioned Dickensian actor. And, though the *Advertiser* doesn't actually mention it, he was invited especially to open the theatre. Lady Dunedin was there merely to lay the stone.

In the letter Bransby Williams makes no bones about the esteem in which he held Frank Thomson. He remembered with fondness his opening the King's and performing there. He offered to return if the Thomson family or friends requested it. He was 84 at the time. And, as well as saying the place held special memories for him, he asked Trixie to give her father a hug for him! I found this very telling about Frank Thomson because it says much about him as a person. His work shows his ability as an architect (and even in that we can spot his altruism) but it's what other people say about him tells us what he was like as a person.

Williams, writing forty-five years after his opening the King's, had intimated this was the best theatre he'd ever performed in. That's quite an accolade.

But if you're ever in the area, it's worth having a look at the South part of the building in St Andrews Street and even having a walk round the back alleyway. There you'll see the incredible amount of windows the dressing rooms were given. This was virtually unique among British theatres. Dressing rooms were invariably crammed in whatever dingy corners were available. Often they were beneath the stage. The rooms the performers were given was really quite revolutionary.

Above the two (stage and exit) doors at the South end is the outline of the scenery dock door. Its step would have been about seven to eight feet from the pavement. The beam of the winch above still remains. In the days when it was in use, scenery was transported to Dundee by train. It was then loaded into trucks which would take it to be unloaded in St Andrews Street. Often this was done on a daily basis! A typical example of that was during the fifties when the Sadler's Wells were producing five or six shows for the week. The companies, not the theatre, supplied the scenery.

Sadler's Wells were actually the last company to play there. They did so for a week during the start of May in 1961. That was the year when the stage shows came to a halt. The theatre -- renamed the Gaumont in 1950 after a takeover by the Rank organization -- was to be reconstructed into a cinema. This was after fifty-two years of performances by famous theatrical and operatic figures. It had also been the home of the Dundee Operatic Society since 1923.

Indeed it had doubled as a cinema and variety hall since 1928. But that was not before it hosted some of the greatest performers and actors of the Victorian and Edwardian ages -- *and* of the later "Georgian" period. (George having ascended to the throne during the following year after the King's opening.) Marie Lloyd, Little Tich, George Robey and Florrie Forde are just a few samples of those performers.

Pantomimes, stand-up comedy acts, jugglers, singers (soloists, duettists, choristers, etc.), all sorts of dancers, gymnasts, acrobats, ventriloquists, conjurers, illusionists, and so on, were appearing there from the earliest years. Many of them were the big names of their day, some internationally famous, though long since forgotten. But nor was the King's slow in attracting the truly great to whom posterity has been especially kind.

The Royal Carl Rosa and D'Oyly Carte companies produced famous operas there. And during that period Harry Lauder and Will Fyffe appeared there. Several of the Royal Carl Rosa and D'Oyly Carte singers were then as famous as their companies. But these days they are known only among the buffs, so not worth my while listing. Though their productions -- still famous -- *are* worth mentioning as are other production and performers who appeared on the King's during those early years.

The Carl Rosa Quartet sang in aid of the Lord Provost's Distress fund on Sunday, 27th March, 1921. The following Sunday a company of Italian opera singers performed a charity concert for the Earl Grey Fund.

The Royal Carl Rosa Opera Company produced the following for the week commencing Monday, February 6th 1922:

Mon, *Faust*; Tues, *Carmen*; Wed, *Cavalleria;Rusticana & Pagliacci*; Thurs, *Samson and Delilah*; Fri, *Tannhauser*; Sat, *Madam Butterfly*; Sat Eve, *Il Trovatore*.

Nearer the end of the same year *The Beggars Opera* was performed on 20th November with the full London Company Orchestra, conducted by Eugene Goossens Snr. And the D'Oyly Carte Opera Company's week -- 18th December to Christmas Eve -- ran as this: Mon, *The Gondoliers*; Tues, *The Mikado*; Wed, *Ruddigore*; Thurs, *Iolanthe*; Fri, *Pincess Ida*; Sat, *The Yeomen of the Guard*; Sat mat, *The Mikado*.

J.M. Barrie's *Quality Street* was staged at the start of 1923, and ran for a week from Tuesday, 3rd January. The *Dundee Advertiser* said of "that purest gem of Barrie ray" that "it went straight to the heart of the large audience..." The *Advertiser* critic certainly thought it an excellent production and one of his statements is worth recording -- especially as it shows not only what people of those times wanted and accepted in a play but their reactions too:

> There is a certain tenderness about the play that makes it very agreeable. The gradually swelling pathos of the closing scene in the first act, when the disappointed girl locks away the wedding dress that will not be needed, was something too fine for words.The poignancy of the incident was not lost upon the sympathetic audience, and the painful silence was just as might have fallen upon the house in Quality Street there more than a hundred years ago.

The Royal Carl Rosa Company returned almost a year to the day to do another week's run -- commencing on Monday, February 5th with *Aida*. That followed with Tues, *Maritana*; Wed, *Lohengrin*; Thurs, *Carmen*; Fri, *Tales of Hoffmann*; Sat, *The Bohemian Girl*; Sat mat, *Faust*.

One of the singers in the Carl Rosa Company at this time was Eva Turner, one of the first British singers to perform all over the world -- and one of the greatest.

The year approached its end, firstly, with a twelve nights run of the D'Oyly Carte Opera Company's productions, starting on Monday 10th December: *The Mikado;* Tues, *The Gondoliers;* Wed, *The Yeomen of the Guard;* Thurs, *Cox and Box & HMS Pinafore;* Fri, *Patience;* Sat, *The Gondoliers;* Sat mat, *Iolanthe;* (Second week) Mon & Tues, *Ruddigore;* Wed, *Iolanthe;* Thurs, *Princess Ida;* Fri, *Trial by Jury & The Pirates of Penzance.* Sat, *The Mikado;* Sat mat, *The Yeomen of the Guard.* These were followed by a week's run of the pantomime *Dick Whittington and His Cat.*

And, as I say, these occurred within the first fifteen years of the King's existence. But the great shows, acts, operas, plays were to continue and the great performers were to continue performing.

The latest and most successful of the London plays was to become a frequent feature there. The first was performed on Monday, September 7th 1925. It was Ian Hay's *The Sport of Kings,* a comedy about racing. It was first produced at London's Savoy only a year earlier by Robert Courtneidge's Number One company. The *Advertiser* called it "...a sparkling piece, which is in the author's best vein."

It was followed, the next week, by another Courtneidge production, *Lightnin'.* Horace Hodges played the main protagonist. This was another which had been a Savoy hit, revived there only a few weeks earlier. And the week following that brought another London hit called *Tiger Cats.* The *Advertiser* called *that* a "really first class show." The two stars were Stephen Ewart and Ida Stratham who were then big London names. It also ran for a week.

The next hit, *White Cargo* came directly on the heels of *Tiger Cats.* The *Advertiser* said that it had taken London by storm and "...the cast will be worthy of the play." It was already running for its second year.

These plays were an excellent start to the winter's programme. And at that point the King's management had made it known they were "negotiating for the appearance of such famous players as Mrs Pat Campbell, Arthur Bourchier, and Henry Baynham..."

As if to celebrate this turn of events a Tea and Supper Room was opened by Lord Provost High. The occasion took place on Monday, 5th October, in what was formerly the stalls waiting-room. The group attending were mainly Dundee public figures, including James Lockhart, one of the directors.

As this event preceded the *Merchant of Venice* -- which was to run for the week -- the provost said that there was "...many lovers of Shakespeare in Dundee and it's to be hoped that the King's Theatre will get the success it deserves... The older pupils of the schools may benefit greatly by a visit to the theatre this week.

This point should not be lost sight of."

He went on to say that many fine shows had been booked for the future and that he hoped the public would appreciate the efforts made for their entertainment.

The Tea and Supper Room was open every night from 6:15 to 11o'clock. Tea and light refreshements were served prior to the entertainment and during the intervals. Supper was served after the end of the performances. Pending demand, dinners could be booked. The catering was run by J.R. Ingram of Lamb's Restaurant. The Lord Provost commended him in his speech as "...one of the city's most pushful businessmen" who "had a brain for development."

Dundee was in for a treat six months (almost to the day) later when Sir Frank Benson's Company did a week's run of Shakespeare. It commenced on Monday, 5th April, with *The Merchant of Venice;* Tues, *Macbeth;* Wed, *Hamlet;* Thurs, *Julius Caesar;* Fri, *Twelfth Night;* Sat mat, *As You Like It;* Sat eve, Sheridan's *School for Scandal.*

The previous Friday the *Dundee Courier* pointed out:

> After an absence of so many years it will indeed be a treat for Dundonians to have Sir Frank Benson and his talented company in the city again. "FRB" as he is generally known, needs no introduction, and to say much about so able an exponent of Shakespeare's work is unnecessary.
>
> It will be sufficient to say that he will open his week with one of his most notable parts, that of Shylock in *The Merchant of Venice* whilst during the week he will also be seen as Mark Antony, Malvolio, Jaques and Sir Peter Teazle. In *Hamlet* and *Macbeth* he plays the small but important parts of the Ghost and the First Witch, leaving the title roles to his leading man, Arthur Phillips...The leading lady is Genevieve Townsend, who is everywhere acclaimed as a leading actress and elocutionist. Of the others in the company it will be sufficient to say that they have all been with Sir Frank for many years, and he has no use for "duds."

About eleven months later (Tuesday 15th March, 1927), after a performance, the orchestra celebrated the eighteenth anniversary of the King's opening with a supper in the Tea and Supper Room.

In 1927, when the Moss Empires took over the King's, control from Dundee was lost. But the great entertainment was not. And the great entertainers continued to perform there. There is not enough room in this small book to list a quarter of the operas and plays staged there nor to name a quarter of the performers. Though one play that was staged there is worth mentioning. It was a thriller called *The Ghost Train.* It had been a bit of a hit at the Prince of Wales theatre in London. It ran at the King's twice nightly for a week, commencing from 8th August 1927. Its writer, Arnold Ridley, ended up more famous than his play -- around forty years later as

Private Godfrey in the BBC series *Dad's Army*.

And before the year ended there was a season of Shaw plays, performed by the Macdona Players Company. The first week, in their daily order from Monday to Saturday, they ran such as: *Pygmalion, Arms and the Man, The Philanderer, Mrs Warren's Profession, The Doctor's Dilemma* and *Fanny's First Play*. The following week the plays ran, from Monday to Saturday, in this order: *You Never Can Tell, Getting Married, Pygmalion, The Devil's Disciple, Mrs Warren's Profession, Man and Superman*.

The *Courier and Advertiser* of October 4th tells us that the first night was a packed house and that the audience was enthusiastic. It went on to say that it was a "happy accident that the autumn holiday coincided with the beginning of the Shavean [sic] fortnight" and that "holidaymakers undoubtedly helped to fill the bumper house". It suggested we could take it as an omen for a successful run.

The ban on *Mrs Warren's Profession* had long since been lifted, hers being the "oldest profession"! The *Courier and Advertiser* of October 7th suggested that one ought to read Shaw's introduction before going to see the play: "otherwise the show becomes a rather sordid affair". Though the writer did state that the Macdona players "did their best with it last night..." And the *Evening Telegraph* critic praised Shaw for having the courage to tackle such a subject, especially as he wrote it thirty years earlier in the Victorian era.

The Macdona Company's greatest achievement at the King's must have been *Man and Superman*. This was the first time the Don Juan in Hell scene was included. It was usually dropped from productions as actors often complained about its length and its difficulty in performing. Esme Percy, a highly esteemed actor and friend of Shaw's, was one of the few actors willing to learn the whole scene. It was through his influence that the scene was included. Margaret Rawlings (an actress of celebrity status virtually till the day she died, aged 89, in May 1996) toured with the Macdona Company and played at the King's. Prior to appearing at the King's the company, which specialized in Shaw plays, had completed a five week run in Glasgow. It was quite an achievement for the 20s period for a theatre company to go around the country without a subsidy.

The following year brought about great changes. March saw a departure from opera and the great plays when a mystery play, *Dracula*, was introduced. The play, commencing Monday 5th for a week, already had a run of over 400 performances in London so it wasn't much of a gamble. It was a Henry Warburton production and featured Wilfred Fletcher and Victoria Kingsley in the cast. These were big names for their day.

That was followed by another popular production, a musical called *The*

Swordsman. It featured D'Artagnan and was really a re-write of the other dramas based on Dumas' *The Three Musketeers*. Carl Brisson played D'Artagnan and his leading lady was Marguerite Ronald, playing the heroine, Constance. It included an operatic chorus of forty.

That was followed the next week by the Dundee Operatic Society's production of Flotow's *Martha* which in turn was followed, by *The Girl Friend*, This, according to the *Dundee Courier and Advertiser* of Tuesday April 10th, 1928, was "thoroughly to the taste of the large and happy holiday audience" and it "received a good reception". The critic went on to say, "A better show than *The Girl Friend* would be difficult to find. The six scenes are brim full of quick action and bright entertainment, and interspersed are some catchy tunes."

A report in the *Courier and Advertiser* of Saturday, June 23rd, showed that far greater changes were about to happen. It mentioned the impending sale of The King's Theatre, for it to be used as a cinema. A further report on Tuesday, July 3rd, in the same paper, told of the plans passed by the Dundee Town Council in relation to the "New Regime" for the King's:

> The approval by the work's committee of Dundee Town Council yester-day of plans for the extensive alterations to the King's Theatre leads to the completion of negotiations for the sale of the house. The scheme entails the remodelling and extension of the entrance hall by taking in a large room in which the booking hall is presently situated, and internally it includes the introduction of a lift from the ground to the gallery, a new cinema box and an organ.

Before the new owners, the Provincial Cinema Theatres, Ltd., took over the building, a thriller and (what I take to be) a couple of variety turns were staged there prior to the final show -- Seymour Hicks in *Mr What's His Name* -- on Monday August 13th.

The Dundee public had been told in advance, through the local press, that the new owners, the Provincial Cinema Theatres, Ltd., intended to present picture and variety programmes, and a play at least once a month. But, under the continued management of R.G. Walker, the stage was only used very occasionally.

So, when it had become more of a variety hall and doubled as a cinema, the tradition of great entertainment -- from great operas to popular modern music and drama -- continued. Where do I begin to name them!? I'll give a couple of examples:

John Hansen performed there for a week, from Friday October 12th, 1959 as Prince Karl in *The Student Prince*. And less than two months later, on Wednesday December 2 of the same year, for two performances, Cliff Richard and the Shadows sang and played to mobs of screaming Dundee teenagers. It showed that things didn't change in that old tradition nearly a decade after Rank had taken over -- and renamed the King's the Gaumont.

It was goodbye to all that in 1961, though when it became a full time cinema.

Dundonians were greeted on the Friday morning of May 19th of that year with the *Courier and Advertiser* headline DUNDEE GAUMONT TO LOSE ITS STAGE. The accompanying article lamented that it was the end of an era for the theatre and told of what was to come.

They mentioned that the Sadler's Wells Opera would have "...the honour of having been the last live players on the theatre's boards." However the Old Vic company were not so fortunate. Their two Shakespeare productions from October 16th to the 21st had to be cancelled. Judy Dench was then a member of the Old Vic.

Their spokesman, Partick Ide, was asked if the company would be willing to perform elsewhere in Dundee. He said, "I welcome the idea. But it would have to be next year. And the theatre would have to seat between fifteen hundred and two thousand."

The Gaumont capacity was 1,400. Nine thousand seats were booked for the the the six days of the Sadler's Wells Company. So, at least the last week did not go out with a fizzle.

It was sad news for the Dundee Operatic Society members. It meant they no longer had a stage for their annual March show. T.J. Wishart, their president, said, "There appears now to be only one other theatre where we might go. The Palace. Even then there is no guarantee we will get it." Arthur J. Millar, the society's vice-president and former musical director called it "A nasty blow." He was worried that it might be the end of Dundee's Operatic Society, stating that was the last thing he wanted to see. He did try to remain stoical by telling the press that his group should just "take it as something that has come along".

Robert Wood, the present manager and who remained when the Gaumont became a cinema, was stoical also and a bit upbeat.

He pointed out the unavoidable economic aspect. "The Gaumont is essentially a cinema nowadays, and it must be up to date. The public now expect that for their money. The loss of a theatre to the city is unfortunate. But it is unavoidable in the circumstances. It would be economically impossible to run as a theatre every week.

"Apart from the impossibility of getting the revenues for live show prices, there aren't the shows on tour to be had now."

To bring in the kind of public that had high expectations for their money Mr Wood explained the procedure.

"We anticipate making the Gaumont a real ultra modern cinema...

"There will be big structural alterations and, unfortunately, it means that the stage will be done away with. A much bigger screen will be put in, and it will be installed right at the back wall; hence the necessity for demolishing the stage."

He also said that the theatre frontage and foyer would also be entirely modernized. And "...there will be other internal improvements, including reseating and redecoration."

Mr Wood then told the reporter that it was hoped work on the Gaumont would begin in a fortnight. The cinema was to be closed for five or six weeks. "Contractors will be working round the clock shifts."

If Robert Wood's stoicism was understandable his concept of "improvements" and "redecoration" proved to be questionable. Those who were pessimistic regarding the changes had every resason to be so. As time so clearly told. The cinema now had luxury seats and a wide screen but all the Edwardian craftsmanship was gone from the auditorium, the ceiling being the exception.

I can remember the changes. For the life of me, I can't remember the seating being any more comfortable. The only thing I can remember, on seeing the many films I did in the modernized cinema, was the films themselves. The enjoyment of merely being in the place was gone. Forever.

IT IS FORTUNATE that much has still been preserved though it cannot be seen. The proprietors, First Leisure, have done a wonderful job building around all of the listed interiors. Shona Duncan, not only invited me into the building, took time to show me around and answered my questions -- as I've mentioned in the acknowledgements -- but she helped me identify and compare remaining design and decoration with photographs I'd been given of the interior.

Once I'd gone through the second entrance she showed me a circular ceiling that had been covered with loose drapery. It was to the left of the entrance, above the Cowgate window side. From another of my photographs, I could identify the ceiling. The drapery is covering a plain, level circle so, if anything, it enhances that part. And, fortunately, the surrounding cornice is still exposed.

Opposite the tables underneath the ceiling is a wall with two "French Renaissance" blind (blocked in) archways, either side of an open one. The pilasters and arches, with Corinthian capitals, are reminiscent of the portals and arches of the upper boxes; but minus the Rococo moulding.

When I asked Shona what was behind them she told me, "The original stairs," then offered to show me them. Naturally, I accepted and she led me through another entrance. We were soon on the original stairs.

I found them unchanged from the Gaumont days. The upper parts of the walls are yellow and the lower parts -- to about the waist height of an average adult -- an almost dark turquoise blue. They were separated by white, wooden, slim corniced beading -- roughly a couple of inches thick. The banister handrails are shiny black. Its balusters (the parts that hold up the handrail) are a gold-painted metal of an Art Deco-ish style. This was possible as the banister (the sum of all the parts) was built during the refurbishment of 1961. The whole feel of the staircase, accentuated by the colours, is very sixties -- especially early sixties. And the banister blends in and contributes to the feel. Between the balusters are panels of blue-tinted streaked glass.

When we climbed to the staircase landing leading to the dress circle we could see the *Art nouveau* windows I mentioned earlier. They are a bit of a surprise because the light from outside makes them stand out quite strongly. Yet they're hardly noticeable from the street. Though they must have been during the dark evenings when the staircase was lit. The lower (square) windows aren't quite so dramatic as they are boarded on the outside. (Those red boards that can be seen from the street.) But the *Art nouveau* designs on them are still identifiable, as the inside of the boards are white.

Each centre pane of the upper half of the windows contains a theatrical symbol. It is surrounded by a wreath of red, blue, two yellow and three or four shades of green leaves. The bottom of the wreath is in the top part of the upper pane. Its left side is to the right of the left pane and its right side to the left of the right one. The top is to the bottom of the top middle. This pane -- like every other one in the whole window -- contains a cross of three lines. A ribbon is twisted around the centre of this cross and falls down to almost touch the top of the wreath at the vertical glazing bar. In the pane either side it rises again to meet the centre of each cross there where it terminates in a looped bow. From each bow hangs a tassle. These are of the style of the wreath's leaves. They also appear in the centres of the crosses on the left and right hand bottom panes of the upper halves of the windows and in the three upper panes of the lower halves. They appear also in the lower panes to the left and right of these. Directly underneath the wreath (the middle pane of the window's upper half) is one tassle which is larger than the others, by way of an extra cluster of small leaves beneath. There are two roughly the same size which appear, respectively, on the centre of the cross on the panes to the right and left of the central upper part of the window. Each of these has a red centre. And they make the outer parts of the centre sides of the wreath. The windows display Thomson's love for and attention to symmetry.

They are greatly influenced by Charles Rennie Mackintosh and are in almost excellent condition. I noticed only one small pane that was damaged. There was a crack with a small hole on one of the lower windows. (Thankfully not a lower part of one of the upper windows.) And, happily, it is a clear pane and easily replaceable.

These are the windows that were over the original canopy. Facing the building from the Cowgate they are the second to fourth windows. The experts I've consulted have no way of knowing at present if any of the other windows had the same design. I suspect they didn't . Their effect is powerful as they slide down to greet the eye of the beholder on ascending the stairs. It is an equally pleasant experience on viewing them from the doors of the dress circle. Thomson must have envisioned the pleasant shock of the playgoer coming out from the auditorium to be greeted by the sight.

Also, another reason I *suspect* they were the only windows with the *Art nouveau* design is because of the symmetry. Looking at the Cowgate elevation from directly in front, it is easy to see that the balance would have been tilted had any of the other windows borne the same design. The original lights bearing the King's name were above the stair windows, in line with the canopy which was in line with the original entrance. At night-time, when it was lit up it would have created a perfect symmetry. These groups were certain to be lit all at the same time. The stair windows have narrower spaces between them than the next set to the immediate West. But, as highly likely as it is, please note that it is still only theory and I am ready to stand corrected.

I showed Shona a picture of a wagon ceiling with a pendant cornice for light fittings and asked her where it could be. This ceiling was made of red panels surrounded by white cornices. Shona reckoned it was above us, but after wandering through what seemed like a maze of corridors, and losing *my* bearings, we weren't able to locate it.

We went as high in the building as was safe. Shona reckoned we'd arrived in the gods. It was difficult to tell as the front of the balcony was sealed off with some kind of material as was the ceiling above us.The steps which had once held seating were about two- to two-and-a-half feet each. I was able to recall that the ones in the gods were much steeper. The tops of the gods seats being level with the feet of those in the seats behind. Then I noticed that the windows for the projectors were behind us. Then I knew we were in the dress circle.

But since then, I've discovered why Shona was convinced there was no other balcony above us. During my researches through back copies of the *Courier* I read an article (May 19th, 1961) explaining:

> ...the gallery (known as the upper circle) will be closed and part of it cut away
> to obviate the beams from the film projection unit being interrupted by the
> floor of the gallery.

The reporter was informed of this by the aforementioned Robert Wood, the

Gaumont manager. Initially, this can seem puzzling as the Gaumont doubled as a theatre and cinema for thirty-three years till then. But the original screen, in use from 1929 to 1961 was a small one hung at the proscenium arch. So, during that period, it was easy to project the beam below the upper circle without casting a shadow. That would not have been possible with the beam for a larger new screen.

As soon as we returned to the ground floor she took me to the basement level. This was entered through the open "French Renaissance" archway where the cafe had been until the sixties. The stairs are now carpeted. But they are divided by central bannisters of a similar design to the upstairs ones, with the same kind of balusters, but without the tinted, streaked glass or the black shiny upper parts on the handrails. Needless to say, these are sixties additions. They lead down to a landing where the original toilets stood and are still usable. The parts of the walls, from about waist height upwards, are mainly large panels. Some of these are pinkish and some yellow, surrounded by white framing. Alternating with those panels are others, about a third in width of the pinkish and yellow ones, with Renaissance style loriat designs on blue backgrounds. Between the white framing of the panels and above and beneath them are the strips of what can be seen of either wall. These are about four or five inches in width and are painted yellow.

The stairs and landings are carpeted, sadly, covering the marble stairs and landings. Thankfully Shona took me through the doors that shut off the lowest part to the public. This is where the staff kitchens are. I could see that the stairs past the doors were Carrara marble -- as a picture of the upper ones showed. Shona pointed out the cracks and chips in them. The upper ones are in a similar condition, thus the carpeting for safety. It's also for safety reasons that the lower parts, then, aren't open to the public.

The lower landing in that part is in either a kind of conglomerate greyish marble or a random mosaic. It was difficult to tell which. It was inlaid with long strips of black marble, making kinds of borders. (The other landings are the same kind of marble and pattern though now covered by carpeting.)

The windows and doorway into the former cafe were pedimented. These were open and scrolled, with Baroque-type heads in between. One of the cafe's main features was its soda fountain. But it wasn't an original part of the theatre, the refreshment places being the bar and Bodega.

One famous addition to the King's during its cinema days was the massive Wurlitzer organ. It used to rise up from under the stage. The organist, Hill Cutler, would be playing it as it ascended in a spiral to stop with him facing the screen where words of a song appeared. A ball would bounce from word to word as the audience sang in unison. So even as a cinema it was pretty classy. Most Dundee cinemas were nowhere near in its league.

Surely the most famous Gaumont organ player was "Aunty Cathie." This lady was well-known in Dundee show business and music circles and better known as Cathie McCabe. The kids club to and for whom she played was collectively known as the *GB Club*. It had formerly been called the *King's Club*. Its name was changed on the theatre/cinema being renamed the Gaumont. And Cathie's most famous rendition to the kids was the club anthem. Some of the songs would change but the anthem remained. My brother-in-law (who can still sing it word-for-word) tells me he sang it in the forties, after the War. I sang it in the late fifties. It was a cameraderie song -- with a touch of the Dale Carnegie philosophy -- which also encouraged the kids to be decent citizens. I can remember bawling out the last lines with a promise that we would be

Greeting everybody with a smile, smile, smile --
Greeting everybody with a smile!

And I can also recall my friends and me thinking ourselves terribly funny by turning our heads around and beaming a huge grin at everyone in sight. Most other kids did it and, no doubt did so every week since the matinees started until the day they finished.

There were other worthies involved with the King's and the Gaumont other than the great actors, divas and other gods and idols. I did try to find out more on Bill Rodgers, the King's first orchestra leader. His daughter, Mrs Margaret Kidd, told me he was well known in his day as a virtuoso. But I'm afraid none of my researches uncovered anything about him, albeit that there is apparently a street in his native town of Kelty named after him. That's one of the sad things about posterity. It's not always favourable to the deserving -- a bit like the other kinds of fame. But Mrs Kidd's lead was welcome. I did find other things relevant to the King's/Gaumont on my searches for information on her father.

The Trust did ask for people with any recollections to contact me. They made their request through the *Courier*. It was kindly featured in *The Craigie Column*, asking anyone with any personal reminiscences or inside knowledge on any kind of worthies involved with the King's to contact me. Unfortunately, the response was low. And, as in the case of Bill Rodgers, the leads were minimal. Scrutinizing programmes, the past columns of music critics, old Dundee newspapers, and books in the local history section of the Wellgate library section led nowhere regarding Mr Rodgers' career.

However, I have uncovered other material which may be used in a later and larger book. We were restricted to size on this edition. So any data or information anyone has relating to the King's/Gaumont,which they think may be of use to the

Trust, would be welcome -- especially characters involved with the King's and odd or amusing stories relating to them. And these characters wouldn't have to be restricted to performers or staff. We'd be happy to hear of any worthies, including members of the public who may have been regulars.

The person to whom this information ought to be passed is Stephen Fraser, at 18 Rockfield Street Dundee DD2 1LD.

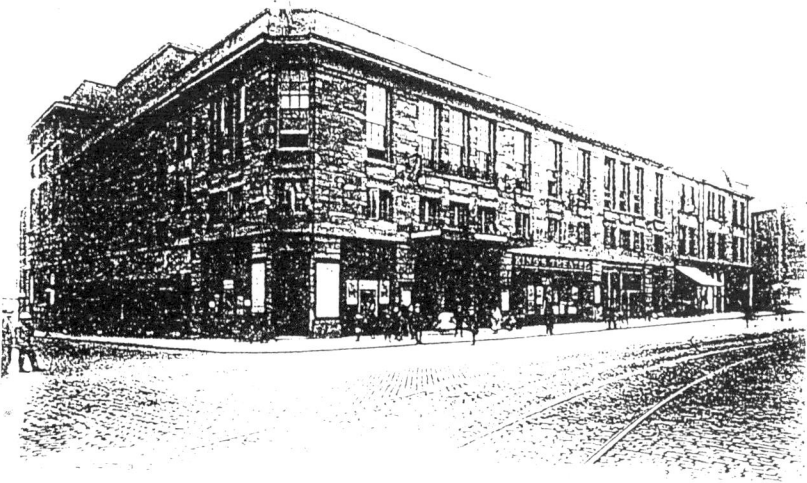

King's Theatre Circa 1910   Picture B

FRANK THOMSON

FRANK DRUMMOND THOMSON was a bit of a prodigy from his childhood .

He started his education at Dundee High School and excelled in mathematics. His headmaster pleaded with him to specialize in that subject. But, even as a schoolboy, his mind was set on becoming an architect.

That's an apt enough career for a young man with a gift for maths. And architecture demands many other skills from its practitioners. Draughtsmanship, an understanding of aesthetics, a knowledge of the history and countless styles of architecture, of the work of other architects, of all the kinds of stones and woods of which buildings are constructed, of various aspects of all the trades involved (bricklaying, masonry, plastering, glazing, plumbing, joinery, gas and electricity work, etc.,), of town planning, geology and geography being just a few.

In other words, an architect has to be an artist, a scientist, businessman and a practical person all in one. Frank Thomson knew that. Even as a boy. But he was not deterred. His determination was to the lasting benefit of his native city -- whether or not her citizens are aware of it!

He knew it because his father was an architect -- one of the most outstanding

Scotland has ever produced. James Thomson was the greatest exemplar any young aspiring architect could have. And Frank had him for a father!

No doubt it was seeing his father's own achievements that encouraged Frank. And perhaps it was his father's tenacity that inspired him. For James Thomson was a David among many Goliaths throughout his career -- and he had to slay many giants of officialdom and bureaucracy. Often he was frustrated in his attempts to make Dundee the city it could have been.

And we wouldn't have much of what he has left to us were it not for his tenacity and determination to challenge narrow-minded councillors and other officials.

It's not too much of a digression here going into the life and work of James Thomson. It is well worth mentioning, albeit briefly, because it is relevant. Though what is really needed is a whole book to be written on this unsung hero's life.

The *Courier* columnist, Jim Crumley, in his book *The Road and the Miles to Dundee*, wrote with enthusiasm and admiration for this man whose "experiences working on post-Improvement Act projects were coloured by the breadth of his vision, a relentless optimism in the face of much scepticism, and a compassion for the working classes of downtrodden Dundee." It's an excellent start.

Soon after Thomson joined the staff of the Burgh Surveyor in Dundee -- when still quite a young man -- he was actually supervising the aforementioned important schemes under the Improvement Act of 1871.

His worth was soon recognized and he was made Assistant Burgh Engineer and, on the death of William Alexander, was appointed City Architect. In 1906 he was given the post of City Engineer in succession to Mackison. So he became the joint holder of the offices of City Architect and City Engineer. In spite of his ability to hold these two offices and his ability to visualize and design amazing architectural projects, he provoked envy. But the mediocre are always envious of the truly talented. The latter unwittingly expose the mediocre.

He was the man who produced the Kingsway "...so that the city might expand advantageously and scientifically ...and get away from the old-fashioned methods." In his work for better housing of the ordinary people he earned a national reputation. As a result of his untiring efforts Dundee took first place in the housing enterprise immediately after the (First World) war. Dundee had council houses built while other Corporations were not past the stage of bickering over the buying of ground.

His obituary notice states that, "In the world of housing the name of James Thomson was writ large, and was regarded with respect. He was one of the stalwarts, and the Board of Health in Edinburgh placed great reliance on his views." And chief officials of the Government Housing Department, publicly stated their indebtedness to and faith in James Thomson.

His greatest monument is the Caird Hall. And even there, masterpiece as it is, he was frustrated by the demands of Caird. Had he not stood up to Caird we would not have had the magnificent pillared front. And it was with great reluctance that he saw the demolition of the Town House. But the stone was in such a bad state that it was becoming dangerous -- as was the stone of the other surrounding buildings.

In 1916 he was elected a Fellow of the Royal Institute of British Architects and President of the Institution of Municipal and County Engineers. In 1922 the offices of City Engineer and City Architect were separated and he became, instead, City Architect and Housing Director, He retired in 1924 but was retained by the Town Council as a consultant.

But those who were envious of his abilities and achievements accused him of self-interest. ALL the records of transactions done by James Thomson testify to a character of the most scrupulous honesty.

Anyway, I mention this to show the legacy to which Frank Thomson had been heir. As James Thomson was determined to change the face of Dundee by getting the working classes out of the narrow lane slums -- which bred the worst diseases of the time -- into wide open-spaced housing among parklands and greenery, we can see that his son followed in his footsteps when he regarded the "least" of the theatregoers and players in his designs.

On leaving school Frank Thomson was apprenticed to a local architect, Thomas Andrew Capon. After finishing his apprenticeship, five years later, he went to London. There he worked for the well-known firm of Niven and Wigglesworth. And he was involved with the plans for the *Courier* building. And it was while working for Niven and Wigglesworth he designed the King's. This he did in his spare time as it wasn't a commission for his firm.

While in London he spent much of his spare time in private study of theatre architecture. He visited many theatres and became an authority not only on the buildings *per se* but on the performers also. He was a man who enjoyed singing and loved to do so with his family.

He returned to Dundee either when the King's was being built or soon after its completion. We don't have exact dates. But he set up business in an office in Castle Street in 1909 -- the year he married and went to live in Cupar, Fife.

In 1911 he entered a competition for the new proposed St John's Cross Church. He submitted three sets of plans for the competition, working on the final details late into the evening of the submission day. He was so exhausted on catching the last train home to Cupar that he fell asleep in the carriage. When he woke up in Edinburgh he had to explain to an inspector what he was doing there with a ticket for Cupar! But such was his dedication to his work.

St John's Cross Church stands in Blackness Avenue. It is reckoned to be one of the most beautiful ecclesiastical buildings in Scotland. It was built during the pastorate of Marshall B. Lang -- who became moderator of the General Assembly. He was brother of the then Archbishop of Canterbury. The archbishop was so taken by St John's Cross Church that he wrote to Thomson praising what he felt was a wonderful building.

When the Town Council bought the Gaelic Chapel in South Tay Street in 1846, it became St John's Cross Church. The congregation remained there till the completion of Thomson's church in 1914. His parents were founder members of the St John's Cross Church in South Tay Street as was D.M. Brown, owner of the famous store in the High Street (now Arnotts).

Thomson also designed Craigiebank Church in 1937. It stands in Greendykes Road. Built in the early Norman style it consists of nave, transepts, choir chancel and organ chamber. Like St John's Cross Church it was designed with a tower. But funds couldn't be found to build either tower. The original designs show just how much of a distinctive part of each church was omitted and how regrettable it must have been for Frank Thomson. The fact that these churches are still impressive and beautiful buildings attests to the ability of the architect.

Arthur Henderson, owner of the Queen's Theatre, asked Thomson to design a building for silent movies. As Henderson had little faith in the "talkies", believing the future to be in live performances, he wanted the building to be suitable for touring theatre companies. It was named the Alhambra and opened in 1929. This was the building in Bellfield Street which became the State cinema in 1941 until it closed in 1968. It then became the the Whitehall Theatre. Perhaps the irony would have pleased Henderson. However, the theatre has an amazing feature not generally known to the public. The dressing rooms beneath the stage were hewn out of solid rock.

In the early part of 1930 Sir James Barrie commissioned a sports pavilion for his home town of Kirriemuir. The designs were to be submitted to an open competition. Barrie chose Frank Thomson's and stated in the remit to the architect that "It should not be ornate or call attention to itself, but should be something that settles down quietly as belonging to the hill -- a Kirrie building, not something from the outside."

He also asked him to include something for the children. Thomson complied and so it is the only sports pavilion in Britain with a *camera obscura*. Thomson also suggested a geographical indicator. That greatly pleased Sir James, and he agreed. The indicator was placed on the verandah to the pavilion's rear. It commands a splendid view of the Sidlaws to the South, the Ochils to the West and the Grampians to the North. The position to twenty-eight hills in all are marked on the indicator. The height of each is given, including their distances from the hill of Kirriemuir.

In those days opening ceremonies were grand occasions. The opening of the sports pavilion (on June 9th, 1930) was one such ceremony. Many dignitaries attended, in top hats and tailed coats, with accompanying ladies equally attired to match the occasion. Part of the ceremony included Mr Thomson presenting Sir James with a golden key to open the pavilion.

Stewart's Cream of the Barley premises in Castle Street were designed by Thomson. It is still generally referred to by this name though it is now occupied by a solicitor's firm. The alabaster light bowls and the stained glass windows depicting the whisky trade are still in position. Thomson helped Sir John Stewart to choose many of the internal furnishings while accompanying him on a trip to London for that purpose. This is a splendid building with a grey granite front and a gate like entrance door of iron and glass.

The Caledon Shipyard offices were also designed by Frank Thomson. They are also quite a feat of engineering as they were built on floating piles.

In his early years as an architect he assisted his father on various projects, the Carnegie libraries to name but a few. The design of the Coldside library -- which was by Frank Thomson -- is particularly revolutionary. Especially the use of bricks in the upper half of the building (which was used for a BBC broadcasting unit). Coldside Library is on the corner of Strathmore Avenue and Strathmartine Road yet the symmetry of this buiding is perfect. The plan is almost fan shaped.

It was perhaps due to his working with his father that a ridiculous rumour was spread around Dundee regarding work he did on the King's Theatre. This rumour was passed off as fact even in otherwise reputable publications.

As the story goes, while working for Niven and Wigglesworth in London, Frank Thomson had been given an inaccurate site survey from his brother. This resulted in the pit entrance being high above the street level. We are told that this was not noticed until the building was completed! And then Frank Thomson appealed to his father, then City Engineer for help. James Thomson then obliged by constructing underground lavatories at the appropriate point as this supposedly necessitated raising the road to the requisite height.

Common sense would cause one to ask how it was the other entrances were at their correct levels. *And* it would require one to accept that the buildings on the other side of the street, at that time, had all their closes and shop doorways high above the street level -- otherwise they'd have been below it on the raising of the street level!

Bill Dow pointed out to me how this slanderous story was quite patently false.

"St Andrews Street was what every interconnecting Street ought to have been. It was a continuous direct incline from the Cowgate at the top end to the Seagate at the bottom. An important point regarding these two streets is that the electric trams went on the Cowgate in 1901 and then on the Seagate around 1904 or 05.

"When you put electric trams on the streets, you have to take out the humps and the hollows, otherwise the trolleys come off. This was obviously done to the Dundee streets though not completely recorded. But the level of the Cowgate was established in 1901, the level of the Seagate no later than 1903. St Andrews Street -- we're talking about its widening -- in 1904.

"Apparently, as a result of relevelling for the trams, there was a bit of a hump or a hollow at the top end of St Andrews Street. And then the street was about half its present width. So, in 1904, the Town Council and the City Engineer decided to take the hollow out. This was absolutely beautifully advertised! Indeed it had to be. When you start playing about with street levels, you can't do so at a whim. Anyone involved in these things realizes that.

"So all the due notices were given regarding reinclining St Andrews Street. Invitations to come to a meeting in December 1904 to lodge objections were advertised. The time was stated. Not a soul objected. That resulted in the City Engineer being asked to sign the plan to show it was correct. He did so. And the City Engineer then was *Mackison*, not Thomson."

The whole West side of the Street was demolished in 1908 but the street had been relevelled almost four years earlier.

"The story is also utter rubbish that the pit door was on the wrong level. There is no evidence to show that the pit door was anything other than at the correct level. When the theatre was completed in 1909, it was given a complete bill of health! I knew several people who were at the opening and they all said there was nothing wrong with the pit door at all. And at that time the gents lavatory didn't even exist.

"The lavatory originally came into the picture in 1901. That's when the City Cleansing Department became worried about a lavatory in Bain Square. It was a cast iron thing they wanted demolished. And they needed to replace it by building a lavatory elsewhere. But every time they found a site they were bombarded with solicitors' letters. It was a perfectly reasonable reaction for people not to want a public lavatory outside their front doors.

"Anyway, the controversy raged for years -- and I mean *years*. And as far as I can establish none of the Thomson's was involved with it. And it was still raging when James Thomson became both City Engineer and City Architect. That was in 1913 -- when the King's was four years old. And as far as I can establish, none of the

Thomsons was involved with it.

"Fed up with the ongoing racket about the Cleansing Department wanting a new Gents lavatory Thomson came up with the idea that it could go in the centre of the now widened St Andrews Street. Its construction started in December 1913 and was completed in February or March 1914. So there were three or four unconnected events which had been deliberately connected to make up this scurrilous story."

It would seem that the "experts" who have written the story as if it were fact did not do the normal kind of research which includes checking one's facts!

David Walker of the Historic Buildings and Monuments Section of the Scottish Development Department in Edinburgh and aforementioned author of *Dundee Architecture & Architects* 1770-1914, wrote to Trixie Thomson in 1986, stating: "I remember your father with the greatest respect and affection : he was one of the best designers in Scotland this century and it is sad that as a result of the depression he built so little between the wars. The significance of so much that he told me has only dawned on me in recent years, and there was so much more I should have asked about."

Frank Thomson was an authority on old Dundee. He loved the outdoor life and loved walking in the country, was a a keen angler, and expert on geology. He worked in his office in 11 Nethergate up till two years before he died. And during the last years of his life he became a keen amateur photographer.

When he died on August 16th 1961, in his 79th year, he was the oldest practicing architect in Scotland, possibly Britain. He survived his wife by three years and is in turn survived by his two daughters Gertie and Trixie (Gertrude and Beatrice).

As these two ladies are justifiably proud of being Frank Thomson's daughters, I will take the liberty of mentioning their own achievements, as I believe Frank Thomson would have been proud of them. And I couldn't imagine either lady themselves mentioning their achievements:

Gertie rose to be Director of the Red Cross. She was awarded an MBE for her life of dedication to that service and on retiring remained Hon. Vice President of the Dundee Branch, completing over fifty years of service. Trixie ran craft fairs for over twenty-five years. She wished to promote talented craftspeople and through the ventures raise money for charity. But her main interest over the past few years has been in building conservation and in stopping developers from demolishing important buildings. By doing so, she follows a family tradition.